Lost and Fou

One Woman's Spiritual Journey in the Desert

Lost and Found in Kuwait

One Woman's Spiritual Journey
in the Desert

Zanne Alder

Alder Publishing

Alder Publishing
Sedro-Woolley, WA

Summary: Memoir - "Under the cover of darkness, I fled Kuwait. In a journey fraught with conflict and adversity, I lost, and then found, spiritual renewal in the Kuwaiti desert."

All names have been changed.

The text of this book is set in 12 point New Times Roman.
All photos by Zanne Alder

The author gratefully acknowledges the sensitive editing of
Andrew Shattuck McBride

... and the early reading and unflagging encouragement of
Dr. Melvin Morse

For my children,

what I love so very much

AUTHOR'S NOTE

The chapter titles are drawn from the
99 Beautiful Names of Allah (Peace Be Upon Him)

Translations come from the website:

https://wahiduddin.net/words/99_pages/wazifa_a.htm

The 99 Beautiful Names of Allah (PBUH)
are the *wazifa* (mantra) used in many Sufi practices.

TABLE OF CONTENTS

Preface

Lost and Found in Kuwait represents a single point of view at a single moment in time. What I find significant is the effect the desert had on my spiritual journey. Any "witnessing" that may seem negative resolves into deep learning for me. For which I am truly grateful.

My experience in Kuwait was narrow in scope. The country itself is small, about the size of New Jersey. I spent my time in the major cities of the country, which all verge on Kuwait City, forming an uninterrupted metropolis. Unexploded ordnance from the Gulf War remains scattered through the desert, limiting travel. After the oil wells were set on fire, 500 large oil lakes formed in the eastern and southeastern parts of the country. Contamination from these lakes left five percent of the country uninhabitable. Sand, oil and soot has hardened into "tarcrete," similar to the photo on the cover.

I am particularly concerned that my writing not be construed as anti-Muslim. (A small example which might be confusing is how staff addressed each other. It was customary to greet adults with their title and first name in formal settings. First names only were used in conversation between colleagues.) As a member of the Sufi Order, I have been performing Islamic practices daily for over 40 years. Universal Sufism is an esoteric teaching rooted in Islamic culture and tradition. It is not universally accepted by Muslims, however. Some view it as heretical, and it is not easily categorized as Sunni or Shia. My experience with Sufism has taught me the beauty of Islam in its purest form, and protected me from forming negative stereotypes about Muslims. While I was in Kuwait, I felt beleaguered by adversity.

Looking back, I realize that only a few individuals created that toxic environment. The vast majority of people I met were open and kind. I thank them for being part of my path.

Salam,

Zanne Alder

Chapter 1

Ya Muid, The Restorer, The Renewer

A Beach in Kuwait

Waiting is always the hardest part. I work all day, alternating between the blistering heat and the frigid air conditioning as I walk between the school buildings and then back into the office. The temperature is 114 degrees and everything feels surreal. I will soon be out of the desert, but none of the people I see today know that.

"Be sure the programs are ready to go to the printer for graduation by the 15th," Janet reminds me. She will be Principal of the Special Needs Department at Shamiya School in Kuwait next year.

"They're all set to go," I tell her; for weeks now she has been assigning me tasks I won't be around to finish.

Finally the day is over. I climb into the overheated Toyota van for the sweaty, bumpy 45-minute ride back to staff housing. It's quiet as the young teachers listen to music or play games on their iPhones. Or sleep off the physical and emotional stress of the day. I silently say good-bye.

We part company in the dust in front of the Soviet-style apartments where we live, and I take the unreliable elevator to the fifth floor. The packing is done; nothing but time between me and the taxi coming at 2:00 AM to take me to the airport. More waiting. Pick-up time comes and goes; no taxi. I am more nervous than usual about reaching the airport on time. I call the driver again. "Yes, yes, I will be there in ten minutes," he assures me. This is one flight I don't want to miss.

The driver calls from downstairs to let me know he's arrived. I slip a letter under the door of the apartment across the hall and pull my suitcases into the elevator with me. The driver and I load them into the trunk next to his box of greasy tools. During the 20 minute ride to the airport, we make small talk. I tip him and head to check in for my flight. I am relieved, and totally at peace as I escape into the night.

Chapter 2
Ya Qabid, The Restrainer

The Pacific Northwest

Having lived my life under the cover of the forests in the Northeast and the Northwest, I don't ooze desert survival skills. I know about the aggravation of biting insects; I prepare for the wildly changeable weather of the mountains; pack the ten essentials. I respect nature and remember it is not Disneyland, but I didn't learn much about sand and heat. If such a person were moving to the desert it would probably make sense to do a little research, make some preparations, even take a few precautions.

In 2012 I left the cover of home and spent a year in the Kuwaiti desert as vice-principal of a special needs department in a large, private school. A year out of the desert, I am turning to the internet for information. (A little late, you say. Well, yes.)

"It's unfortunate that many people equate deserts with a hostile environment that conspires against human life," says *DesertUSA.com*. Seriously? DesertUSA, the desert *does* conspire against human life! There is no water, no vegetation, no shade, and plenty of scorpions, sand cobras, and heat. Brutal heat. And dust storms.

I didn't find much information on the Kuwaiti desert, although it is considered the hottest country on earth. People cluster in and around Kuwait City, probably because of all the undetonated ordnance scattered about, remnants of the Iraqi invasion. I did find a video of truck tires melting on a city street.

DesertUSA advises: "Respect the heat. If water is limited, keep your mouth closed. Do not talk, eat, smoke, drink alcohol or eat anything salty. Limit activity." I can identify valuable advice when I see it. Learning to keep my mouth closed seems like good advice in almost any situation, although I admit to being a slow learner on that one. Not smoking, drinking or eating salty things are good rules of thumb for health. And as I get older, I don't object *too* much to limiting my activity.

"The basics of desert survival?" DesertUSA goes on, "Prepare for the worst. Control panic. Use your brain." I can't imagine better preparedness for my year in Kuwait than these three, short sentences.

More desert wisdom from *Ghostwoods.com*, a website for fiction writers: "There are no distractions, giving deserts an association with clarity, revelation and purity ... These areas are brutal, but they call upon the deepest reserves of a traveller's will. In these struggles, there is no barrier to the heavens, no distractions or comforts to distract the soul from its communion."

Yes, all this and more.

My calling in the work world has always been the

well-being of children. I am a lifer in the school system, working there successfully and happily for 30 years. I taught special education most of that time, specializing in students with behavioral issues. I just loved those wild boys (they were mostly boys) who were so honest, and acted out to be sure they got the support they needed. Sometimes, if kids were too withdrawn, we would try to draw them out, preferring a tantrum to a silent child hiding, but not growing. I developed an adventure-based counseling program that used challenge ropes courses and gave me a chance to see children at their collaborative best. I provided counseling to kids in elementary, middle and high school to prevent suicide, and alcohol and other drug abuse. Life was challenging and sweet.

By the time I was in my 50's, however, I was running out of steam at work. Rebecca Anhorn did not write a book about education entitled *The Profession That Eats its Young* for nothing, and she was not referring to gorging on students. Forty-five percent of all teachers leave education within 5 years. 20,000 new hires quit before June of their first year. The statistics are about double for special education. (Quoted in *Delta Kappa Gamma Bulletin*, Spring 2008.)

I worked an additional 10 years in education, but not quite so happily. Class sizes were going up, pay was going down. My last class had 28 first and second graders in it; we literally could not fit in the room together. Over a period of years I had watched a mental health crisis grow among our children; it grew without being acknowledged, let alone addressed. Pre-school children came to school dropping the "f" bomb. They had to be explicitly taught how to play with cars and kitchens. One of our second graders was so neglected that he planned to kill himself, and had access to the means to do so. Those are the ingredients for a call to Child Protective Services. The law requires that the agency investigate the situation within four hours. When I called the worker a week later to follow-up he said, "Oh, how is that student doing?"

"That's what I am calling to ask you."

"I haven't been over to interview him yet."

Another student had been abandoned by drug addicted parents, and, at four years old, tried valiantly to care for his siblings who were two and three. Still another had been given medication for ADHD that didn't seem to be working. We facilitated his case review with wraparound services including the county mental health agency; he had bipolar disorder. ADHD meds horribly magnify bipolar symptoms in children. His parents finally understood why, when told it was bedtime, he tore the entire house apart.

There were boys and girls who were neglected and exposed to drugs and alcohol in utero; others who were physically and sexually abused. Any one of these conditions results in changes in the physiology of the brain, leading to difficulties attaching to others. The kids don't learn to care about and relate to others. They can't regulate their emotions. They don't notice how their behavior affects others, and don't feel connected enough to care. Violence erupted frequently.

Thirty percent of our students were coping with serious mental health challenges. They were wonderful kids with legitimate, but very high needs. Counselors might see them once a week if all went well. Teachers worked with them in large groups every day, all day, day in and day out.

I had to impact these issues; I was passionate about it. All children deserve the absolute best services we can provide. Nothing is more important. Kids are innocent, and clearly do not bring these problems upon themselves. There were things schools could do that didn't cost money, such as teach respect by modeling it in real life situations, build strong teams with parents to work in the best interests of their children. I worked hard implementing restorative justice practices in the classroom. The kids and I aired problems and found ways to repair the harm that had been done. We met the needs of the person hurt, the one who did the hurting and their friends and family who were, of course, affected by the incidents. (The kids actually chose to do this rather than have extra recess time.) This helped a lot, but there still was not enough of me to go around. The needs were too high and the resources too scarce.

Because of my training and work in counseling, I knew what these students needed to grow, but there was no way public schools could provide it. We needed a much smaller student/staff ratio. (Washington State, where I was working, has the third highest student/staff ratio in the country.) We needed on-site, intensive counseling services. We needed to help parents understand what life is like for their children and what kind of support can help their children thrive. We needed to help children understand how their life traumas could result in behaviors even they found baffling. With this knowledge, they could stop thinking they were crazy and learn different coping strategies.

None of that was happening. If I sound extreme, I can only say this was my reality in public school. Budgets were cut every year for special education for at least 27 years in my state. More recently all budgets were slashed; teachers received pay cuts year after year, counseling services were discontinued, professional development budgets eliminated. And yet everyone seemed to think things were fine in public schools. Everyone has been a student, and assumes they know what it is like. But unless you have taught during the last few years, you do not know the challenges schools and teachers are facing without financial or moral support from many of our communities.

I seriously believed that I could be – in fact, needed to be – the catalyst for changing the enormous public school system. But with the world economy collapsing around our ears, meaningful change in schools became nearly impossible. As our superintendent remarked, "We are trying to fix the plane while it is in flight." We were just trying to stay aloft. I began to see my job as un-doable. It created enormous stress for me as I continued to try and do a perfect job with 28 precious students.

Chapter 3
Ya Khaliq, The Creator

On the Steps of the Lincoln Memorial

Y ou might wonder why it was up to me to fix the public school system. That hubris grew out of my childhood.

When I was a kid, I lived more in my right brain and the present moment, as I suspect we all do. I had a beloved make-believe friend named Johnny, a girl, who was my constant companion. Each member of my family opened doors for her, and made sure she was comfortably seated. No one sat on Johnny, that was just rude. Johnny came along when we drove out to the Midwest every summer to visit our grandparents. I took tons of photographs of her. Somehow those photos never came back from the drugstore.

Other miraculous things happened when I was living happily and innocently in the extraordinary present. For example, I knew my toys were alive. I had proof. Many was the morning I woke up to find Ginny

Doll in a completely different place than where I had left her the night before. No one had been in the room, so the obvious conclusion for any right-thinking person was that Ginny Doll came alive after I went to sleep. She had her fun during the night; if only I could watch! When morning came, she perched wherever she landed, pretending to be just a doll, hoping I wouldn't notice she was in a different spot. (I think the movie, *Toy Story*, may owe me some royalties.)

As a child, some of my experiences were challenging and frightening. You won't catch me wishing to go back to my youth. It wasn't just that toys moved about my room at night. Every single evening, as the room became darker and darker, a witch took possession of my hall tree. What had been an innocent collection of bathrobes, shirts and dresses in the daylight morphed into a hunched-over witch waiting for me to make one wrong move. Every night I lay down on my bed, facing the hall tree, keeping a careful eye on that witch.

I believed in the Easter Bunny and Santa Claus and tooth fairies and all the usual, wonderful beings of childhood. I existed in the present without worries or plans. It was heavenly for a few years. But it wasn't to last; there comes a time when families start to worry if you drag your invisible friend, Johnny, with you everywhere. There comes a time when you have to become acculturated and socialized to the larger world.

Then your family helps you. My family's story taught me that we belonged to a *Different Clan* than everybody else. It was said with humility and good humor, knowing we were kind of strange. We did not conspicuously consume like the others in our neighborhood. We were more serious, more interested in making the world a better place. It slowly dawned on me that being *Different* carried a flavor of *better.* Although we joked about it, our *Difference* was actually superiority. I think my head swelled up a little bit.

My parents' help was a mixed blessing. Their admirable viewpoints were always washed down with copious amounts of alcohol. Their behavior was unpredictable and neglectful, and my brothers and I were left to fend for ourselves.

Without real guidance from my parents, I found myself standing on one side of a glass wall, looking through to where the other kids were playing. I needed to live up to being *Different,* which I read as *perfect.* That's a tough bar to clear, especially from your right brain, and it means leaving the world of the present in the dust. Fortunately we have compulsory education to teach us how to think with our left brains.

And I was good at that. Not as good as some, but I could synthesize information easily. The ability to make connections served me well in rational, analytical tasks. And that was the world I lived in. My grandfather went from being a horse-and-buggy doctor making house calls to seeing a man walk on the moon. Science was definitely the religion in our household, with its accompanying belief that people could accomplish anything they set their minds to. The world was a rational, reasonable place full of problems that should, could, and would be solved by rational, reasonable people. And I, of the *Different Clan*, was tasked with solving these problems.

Although I put up a good front, I didn't feel the least bit confident that I would be found worthy. Instead, my stomach knotted in fear; any minute something could expose me as normal and inferior. I would be cast out of the *Different Clan* forever, left to find my own way in this bewildering world. To fend off that threat, I wholeheartedly threw in with the left brain analysis of the school world; in fact, over-analysis became my drug of choice. I moved out of my right brain and into my left, leaving Johnny, imagination and spontaneity behind. With a clear mandate to fix the world, yesterday and tomorrow became my focus; today, not so much.

Spirituality added another layer to my already heavy responsibilities to the world. My path to spirituality, however, was unconventional. My family chose Science as religion for good reasons. My mother summed it up best when she said, "I can't go to a church where the minister says, 'Love thy neighbor,' but allows no black members." This was the late 50's and early 60's in Washington, D.C. We still had "colored" and "white" drinking fountains. As a result, I grew up with self-proclaimed atheists.

It was occasionally embarrassing if someone asked me what religion I was. Everyone went to church or synagogue in those days, although some religions were more acceptable than others. (Before John F. Kennedy was elected, a Catholic president was unheard of.) So when asked what religion I was, I would say Methodist, the church my mother belonged to when she was growing up. My friend answered enthusiastically, "Really? Me too. Which church do you go to?"

"Which church do *you* go to?" I parried, and then claimed the other one as mine. Lying in the name of religion – never a good thing. And the only lie I told until I was 13 and tried to get into a movie theater for a child's price.

"When's your birthday?" they grilled me.

Easy. "February 1st."

"What year?" They were ruthless.

I paid full price for the ticket.

I grew up without a religious education of any kind. We were hardworking humanists, but not religious.

I did not follow in my parents' atheistic tradition, however. Simple, left-brained logic pulled the plug on that. I was the youngest in the family for 11 years. I have two older brothers, who have always been nice to me, but my mother and I still felt our gender was under-represented. She had one of those surprise pregnancies when I was 11. I so wanted a sister, and began to pray to God nightly, earnestly, fervently. My sister, Emma, was born. I was a believer. That may sound flippant, but to me there was a clear causal relationship. I prayed for a sister, I received a sister. I owed God big-time.

As I applied the rationality that came through acculturation to the baby news, I was bound to acknowledge God's role in allowing Emma into our family. It was, therefore, logical that I believe strongly in God. For some reason, however, I believed that S/He took care of everyone on earth except me. Although I had membership in the *Different Clan*, I didn't really deserve it. I would have to keep proving my worth by myself. Help was not a luxury I could rely on. Perhaps I had some fatal flaw that required me to negotiate life's puzzling ways on my own. Another strange permutation o f *Different* morphing into *better:* only the ordinary receive help. At the same time I feared I just plain wasn't good enough, my swelled head crowed, *I can do this alone.* God laughs!

When I got older, having a non-religious family was downright convenient. Every week huge arguments erupted between parents and teenagers all across D.C.

"I'm not going to church."

"I'm not going to synagogue."

"Yes, you are!"

My parents were extremely tolerant about religious leanings; they didn't care if I was hanging out with atheists, Catholics, Christians or Jews. (Other religions were not represented in our community.) A major stressor that most of my contemporaries struggled with was simply not an issue at my house.

Political divides of the time also caused rifts to arise. Tensions ran high around the Vietnam War, the Civil Rights Movement and the first Earth Day. Fights over politics dominated many relationships between adolescents and their parents. Not a problem in our household. My father appeared on radio shows opposing the Vietnam war long before it had even registered on most people's radar. He took my friend, Linda, and I to our first anti-war demonstration; my mother was so proud. The events taking place as I came of age cemented my belief that society was undergoing a sea change, and that I could be, and needed to be, part of the significant progress of the human race. The *Different Clan* would help move our country into peace and compassion. After all, we stopped the Vietnam War, didn't we?

Life was intellectually and idealistically very rich. I loved the deep discussions during Experimental Education Week at our high school, complete with classes by poet Allen Ginsburg. Yet there were holes in my understanding, and adolescents can't stand not knowing everything. I stumbled on this crack in my wisdom as I delved into literature; there were so many symbolic references to the Bible that just flew by my secular understanding. I felt a certain lack in my life that I didn't know how to describe.

About that time, I started reading books on philosophy, Hinduism and Buddhism, and authors like Jean-Paul Sartre and Hermann Hesse. The spark that was ignited by God delivering me a sister burst into flame. The big questions of the meaning of life and my purpose for being here resonated strongly. Viewpoints that centered around family, service, meditation and peace drew me like a bear to honey.

Fast forward to the relationship between the father of my children and myself. Ben is a remarkable man. I loved him deeply. He was also a member of the Universal Sufi Order (now called the Inayati Order, *inayat* meaning "kindness" or "grace"). The Sufis are credited with creating the story of the blind men and the elephant and inventing chess. They are sometimes described as the mystical branch of Islam. Ben wanted to share his enthusiasm about something that was meaningful to him, and we went to seminars, weekend retreats and lectures. Eventually, I was initiated into the Order.

There were many things that appealed to me in the way Sufism was being taught in the West. Pir Vilayat Inayat Khan was the teacher with whom we studied. According to what I was taught, everyone ends up in the same place; some go with their eyes open and some with their eyes shut. None of this, my group goes to heaven, but the rest of you burn in hell for eternity. I can't imagine a God that would do that. The universality of religions was recognized and celebrated in worship.

Differences between religions were attributed to the historical times in which they arose. Each religion simply spoke in a language that could be understood by the peoples and cultures of the time. But below the surface, the *Message* remains. Or, as John Prine sings, "All them gods is just about the same."

I loved the emphasis on brotherhood and sisterhood, compassion and good works. I worked hard to hone my new tools of meditation, and become a better, less judgmental person. All of which would help me fulfill the promise of the *Different Clan*. Although Sufism appealed strongly to my idealistic self, there was one aphorism that escaped me. Pir Vilayat said, "Shatter your ideals upon the rock of truth." Seriously? Are you kidding? My ideals are the best part of me. Don't worry, life teaches with relentless compassion.

Chapter 4

Ya Haqq, The Truth

My Daughters and I at Fort Worden, Port Townsend

The first shattering came when I had to divorce Ben, whose relationship with the bottle was stronger than his relationship with our family would ever be. I had a strong passion for providing my children with two parents and having a close, intimate relationship myself. I stayed with him for almost 20 years. But it became clear that my ideal was causing more harm than good to both the girls and myself, and probably to Ben as well. Sri Nisargadatta Maharaj, an Indian yogi, reminds his followers that "passion is painful; compassion never." My passion hurt like hell.

So I raised my two children alone, and I must say they are outstanding human beings. They are kind and funny, smart and compassionate. I would choose to hang out with them over just about anybody else in the world. They are my life's work and my most valuable contribution to the world. And I am quite certain I could never have done this without the strength and insight I gained from my spiritual life.

25

During this time, I lost touch with my Sufi teacher, although I continued to do my practices daily. I meditated on the Divine Qualities as represented by the 99 Beautiful Names of Allah (PBUH.) These meditations attune the practitioner to qualities of compassion, strength, mercy, whatever you need to develop within yourself. Like so many traditions, the Chisti Order works with breath, vibration and sound. Given that the core of the physical being is vibration, motion and movement of protons and electrons, it makes sense that a physical being can adjust its state through vibration. It is an act of harmonizing, literally tuning one's body to the Divine. Many Arabic words contain an element of what they name. For example, the word for water sounds like running water. Such close ties between sound and meaning help with this attunement.

My teacher charged me with practices to develop uncompromising truth, no insignificant task. The attunement counteracted my tendency to see people as they could be instead of as they were. It can be a gift to mirror potentialities for others, but a trap if I depend on those potentialities to materialize. I had been trapped in the beauty of who Ben could be; I did not see the reality until I had ruthlessly practiced witnessing truth.

Truth is a hard master, so another practice offered me compassion. Compassion served as a balm to my fears that I was an unsuccessful member of the *Different Clan*. I found some practices came more easily than others. I was adept at those that occurred on the exhalation, where I was absorbed into the One Being – and struggled with the others that emphasized the potential divinity of my singular self. It was easier for me to imagine being engulfed in the ocean of the

One than as an individual drop of water with its own existence. Clearly, this was related to having lived in alcoholic families all my life, where individuals must subjugate themselves to the larger system. It was not acceptable to tend to my own needs, challenges or joys.

Part of what kept me going through the hard times was the practice that tuned me to restoration and revivification. After being shattered, I needed to rebuild from the inside out. Could I trust my judgment in other relationships? Did I have the stamina to work full-time and raise my children? Was I fatally flawed somehow? My practices enabled me to retool for a new and very demanding life. I did not think for one minute that I had the wisdom myself to know what qualities to develop. That is what a teacher is for, and I am grateful every moment for the guidance I received.

About fifteen years later, another bomb went off as the marriage I had viewed as my second chance blew up in my face. The shrapnel was everywhere; the pain of the shattering nearly unbearable. I was devastated and destroyed, beleaguered and betrayed. (The story was so horrific the Montel Williams television show called, and asked me to come on the program to cry and rend my garments. I declined.)

Worst of all, I was without hope. The cockeyed optimist ran out of hope, and, for the life of me, I could not figure out how to live without it.

Knowing I needed help and support, I began attending Quaker meeting in my little town of Port Townsend, Washington. The Quakers, or the Religious Society of Friends of the Seekers of Truth, have many points in common with the Sufis. Their silent meeting for worship became a weekly mini-retreat for me where

I cried and replenished my well. Today someone asked me, "What do Quakers believe in anyway?" This is a notoriously difficult question to answer, especially in unprogrammed meetings like ours. Neither Sufism nor the Religious Society of Friends requires any adherence to dogma.

A Quaker First Day is filled with silence. Our meeting was small enough that we sat in a circle as a group of equals. There is no minister and no service. We trusted in a personal connection to God and the existence of continuous revelation. We waited for the "still, small voice within" to provide guidance; for God, the Great Mystery, the Universe to lead us in a productive direction. If I felt compelled to speak during the silence, as though I couldn't *not* speak, I stood, said a few words, and then settled back into silence. If I was not pushed, I remained silent. Perhaps someone else would speak. This was our vocal ministry, one Quaker to another. Ideally, we were not sharing opinions or thoughts, instead a message came through us that might provide insight and comfort, for ourselves or for others.

The goal of both the Sufis and the Quakers and is not to "create" reality, which speaks of the ego being in charge, but to follow God's leadings and harmonize with reality. Sufis die to their egos in order to be reborn in harmony with the Divine. "Here I am, God, take me," I say. Then I duck because I'm not sure exactly what God might have me do next.

Quakers see "that of God" in everyone, and hold everyone and every situation "in the light." They pride themselves on "speaking Truth to authority." They are frequently the truth-tellers who say the things no one else will, a role I end up in everywhere I go.

One day, I sat in a meeting to discuss political action to increase peace, ensure right use of resources in the world and promote justice, all historically Quaker issues. I was there even though I gave up on politics as a solution years ago. Out of the blue, in the middle of a political pep talk, I was given the key to hope. This tireless activist said to those of us with flagging hearts, "Hope is not something you have or don't have. It is something you practice." Now that was something I could do; I could practice hope.

I quickly discovered why Quakers are called "Friends." This small group of people did not know me. Yet I knew immediately they would help if and when something overwhelming threatened to drown me. They became my community of faith. They listened to my anguish about the tragedies I witnessed everyday at school. They supported me as I struggled with the secondary trauma that comes from being inundated with other people's heartbreak, the heartbreak the children were cloaked in as they came to school every day. Despite my *Differentness*, all my attempts at perfection, all my love and dedication, I was not meeting the needs of the students I served. I was not burned out. I was compassion fatigued.

What to do? One of my litanies is, "I can only complain if I'm willing to work toward resolving the complaint." Otherwise I am choosing to stay in the mess I claim to revile. It's cognitive dissonance. Frankly, no one wants to hear it. I became tired of my own righteous indignation.

I tried various things to make work more doable. I took different jobs in different schools. I investigated changing careers. But I had a mortgage to pay, and any new career would not pay enough to cover that mortgage. Finally, a friend of mine obtained a job teaching overseas. A thought loosened in my mind. *Oh, yeah, I used to talk about doing that when my kids were grown.* I had many friends who had adventured abroad, and they had fabulous experiences. I needed a bridge to retirement which was at least five years away. Tax-free work in international schools, well-behaved students and families that still respected education and teachers? It sounded like the perfect bridge. Clearly, the time had come.

Chapter 5
Ya Mu'akhkhir, The Delayer

North Beach, Port Townsend, WA

Numerous organizations connect teachers with international schools; I signed up with one and headed to San Francisco for a job fair. Job fairs are often described as speed dating for interviews. "You don't always get a job at the fair," the organizers counseled us, but I ignored that advice. I really wanted to come home with a job in hand. I was desperate and honestly didn't know how I could survive another year in public school.

Noticing the beginnings of a cold, I took a shuttle from the airport a short distance to the job fair. Walking into the fancy hotel right on the water, I felt like a country bumpkin. I realize that "fancy" is in the eye of the beholder. I lived in a tiny town of 8,000 people. We wore blue jeans and let our hair go gray. Now, I changed into my interview clothes, ready to walk into a very different world. Excitement bubbled in my stomach as I set forth to talk my way into a job.

There were fewer schools at the fair than the organization had anticipated, but I got a sizable number of interviews. I had an offer in hand after the first one, a job in Kuwait. More excitement! I was a bit dubious about this school after I discovered that it had not registered to be part of the interview event. The interviewer just showed up and talked to people in the hotel bar. He was a job fair crasher. Happily, I was particularly impressed by a newly appointed superintendent at Shamiya School, also in Kuwait, that provided both bilingual and special needs programs. Historically, this has been unusual in international schools, which generally serve affluent, high-functioning students. People with differences, well, they're on their own.

We met in the superintendent's hotel room; that's not shady, just how these fairs operate. He had obviously read my resume before the interview, which was impressive in and of itself. Although I was looking for a teaching position, he told me he would push me toward administration. *Oooh! It was such a compliment;* I swelled with pride. *Being seen and recognized feels so great*, I crooned to myself.

Despite the lift to my ego, I said, "I don't really want to do administration." This was a conversation I'd had with several administrators over the past 16 years. I was sorely tempted by the opportunity to make change, but I didn't really want to go back to school to get an administrative credential. Two Masters Degrees is already excessive, and I was still raising my kids. I had vowed not to sacrifice my own children in the name of someone else's. And I shuddered at the thought of being the bad cop with parents, a role that principals universally hate.

The superintendent offered me a position doing academic testing as a school psychologist. I went back to my room to mull. *School psychologist would certainly slow down my pace after classroom teaching. But I would be so bored, giving the same tests over and over again. I've been giving the Woodcock-Johnson Tests for Academic Achievement for 37 years. Administration? In a school without behavior problems, where people still respect and value education and educators?* It was starting to sound interesting.

I slid a note under the door of the superintendent's room, saying that I'd like to know more about the administrative position he had in mind. Half an hour later, we were talking again. "I have a bunch of teachers sitting around drinking coffee and handing out worksheets," he told me. The hook was offered. "The principal's OK. But I want you to come in and shake up this department." Oh, appeal to my idealistic heart! The hook set deeply in my cheek.

"What's the student population like?"

"You'd be working with the whole gamut, students with mild learning disabilities to those with severe intellectual disabilities. We are not a behavior modification program, and we do not accept students with physical disabilities or severe behavioral problems."

"I don't have experience with students with intellectual disabilities."

Not a problem.

Hmmm. I would actually have authority; most of my positions loaded me with responsibility, but gave me no authority. Hmmm. No behavior problems. Maybe I could actually work on staff development; I loved those years of professional development I did. I took the bait. All my hubris and hope leapt to the fore, and I signed on for the job. I was going to help Shamiya School turn itself around. It was the chance of a lifetime and I was thrilled.

And a little puffed up. "No, actually," I said to people who inquired, "I'm not going to teach, I'm going to be Vice Principal of Special Needs. I'm hoping to do a lot of staff development." *Was that the self-satisfaction of the* Different Clan *in my voice? And the hope of the idealist who sincerely wants the world to be a better place.*

I returned home to four more months of school in a classroom full of beautiful students. My cold had morphed into a full-blown sinus infection, and I started a course of antibiotics, which trashed my intestinal tract. I kept eating yogurt and waiting for my system to regain its homeostasis. But it didn't. Two months went by, and finally I returned to the doctor. It turned out I had an intestinal parasite. I hadn't even left the country yet, and I had an intestinal parasite! Just as that was getting straightened out, I contracted Lyme disease. I struggled weakly through the last two months of school.

I had not originally had the Middle East in my sights; it didn't seem like the best pick for a single woman. But both job offers I received were in Kuwait, and I was determined to leave the U.S. I spent the summer reading up on Arabic culture. I had met a Pakistani-American woman at the fair who recommended some books for me. We talked about Islam and my involvement with the Sufis when we were supporting each other through the interview process. Ilma said, "Oh, they'll love you in the Middle East." And I was looking forward to seeing if what I had been taught in the United States bore any resemblance to Islam in Kuwait.

I haven't talked much about the Sufi practices I do. People might assume I was in a cult. My teacher drove a beat-up old Subaru, not the Mercedes Benz of cult leaders. I think I was safe. It gets even trickier to talk about in the Middle East where conflicts between Shia and Sunni are involved. And I was not especially knowledgeable about where Sufism would fall in that debate.

In reading the books Ilma suggested, I learned a little about the cultural differences I would encounter. I read there is a tendency in the Middle East to have a big confrontation around a conflict, but never really do anything to resolve the issue. I encountered this phenomenon with students, families and staff in American schools. It was a tough one for me. I expect people to recognize problems and work to solve them. And I wondered if the principal of Special Needs at Shamiya School was as interested in change as the superintendent. This would either be my dream job or the job from hell.

I started paring down my belongings, keeping just enough to furnish a small apartment or house when I came back in five years. Things I had once cherished (all the driftwood I'd lugged back to my yard) no longer mattered. Though I'm not a huge keeper, the sorting left me feeling lighter.

The paperwork required to get a resident visa in Kuwait was confusing; I often got completely contradictory instructions from the school as to how to go about things. For a rule-follower like myself, that was cause for frustration, anxiety and a fair amount of money in unnecessary fees. But I knew this was not unusual. It would pass.

I emailed Barb, the principal I would be working with, asking her to describe her hopes for the Special Needs Department, its strengths and weaknesses. "Looking much to seeing you," she wrote back. I couldn't tell if she was a native English speaker or one of the Arabic staff. I was eager to know more about the situation I was headed into, but Barb wasn't talking. Waiting is not my strong suit.

The summer dragged by, with no word that the school had booked my flight. I prepared myself for leaving friends by slowly withdrawing; goodbyes are so hard. I paid last visits to favorite local places. I walked the beaches, but didn't collect shells or rocks or driftwood. I kayaked, reveling in the green, the wildlife, the quiet. I watched bald eagles soar and sea otters float on their backs. I stared at snow-covered Mount Baker, my favorite of the Washington volcanoes. I waited, and waited, and waited for this new chapter of life to begin.

Chapter 6

Ya Mubdi', The Starter

Faculty Housing in Kuwait

The email came on August 17. I was flying to Kuwait in two days! Normally, I prefer to plan five to ten years out. Two days? Are you kidding me?

I moved through time at warp speed, packing, organizing, closing up accounts. Feverishly I loaded my belongings into a storage unit, hoping the Pacific Northwest moisture and rats wouldn't invade. My constant companion was a nagging little voice that warned, "Something is missing."

Enough meds for a year? Check. Appropriate clothes? Check.

Plane Tickets? Check.

I'm not going into the wilderness. There are stores in Kuwait.

All my life, I'd listened ardently to other people's stories of travel. Friends who taught in exotic places like Cambodia and the United Arab Emirates telling me what a great gig it was. But me, I have a homebody streak. I had never even been out of the United States before. No, wait, I have crossed the border into Canada. I've seen a lot of the U.S., wonderstruck by the variety of intense natural beauty. And that was enough for me. Others are drawn to Europe; I was content at home. And at the same time, curiosity about all the different ways people find to live grabs me.

So now, improbable though it seemed, I was heading off to the Middle East. I was going and I was going big. To a location, climate and culture completely different from anything I had ever known. And though my nerves quivered with uncertainty over customs, visas and other travel procedures, I was not the least bit afraid. Staying in my old job – overworked, overwhelmed and depressed – was what terrified me.

Port Townsend's isolation is what keeps it beautiful, but it makes for one hell of a trip to the airport. My youngest daughter, Addie, and her sweetheart helped me load three suitcases and two big boxes of teaching materials into a pick-up truck. We started off for the airport. We drove down the Olympic Peninsula, and crossed the world's longest floating bridge built over tidal waters. We traversed the Kitsap Peninsula, falling silent as it became harder to find things to say.

For the entire 30 minute ferry ride, we silently soaked in Mount Baker, Mount Rainier, the Olympic Mountains and the Cascades. I said goodbye to the Pacific Northwest. On the Seattle side of the Salish Sea, we took I-5 for the last leg to the airport. Three hours after leaving the house, we arrived at SEATAC. Three hours down, 21 to go.

Addie dropped me off at Departures. My heart in my throat and tears in my eyes, I hugged Addie goodbye. *A whole year before I can see her again. And she's still so young. I hope I'm doing the right thing.* My emotions were reeling.

Shakily, I checked in for my flight on Etihad Airlines. I'd never even heard of Etihad Airlines. Next, a three hour wait until boarding, plenty of time to ache for Addie and Lily, my other daughter who lived across the continent and couldn't be there to see me off. Plenty of time to worry about visas and customs. *Oh, my god, that pesky little voice was right! I don't have contact information for the school. I get there in the middle of the night, and I don't even know the address of the apartments.* Now I would worry that no one would meet me at the airport in Kuwait. This is what happens when you don't plan five years ahead.

It will work out, I reassured myself. And in fact, that's one of the things I love about getting older; I have enough experience with things working out that I can detach and trust. I settled into my book to wait.

Life, I've noticed, tends to keep me humble, usually in spite of myself. I am of an age that airplane travel is not as easy or comfortable as it used to be. Some of that I cynically blame on the airlines and the reduction of legroom in the planes, but some of it has to be acknowledged as the aging factor. My plan is to age gracefully, but I did feel a bit self-conscious pulling on my support hose before boarding the plane.

Finally, I walked onto the Etihad jet and left Seattle, as prepared as one can get for a 14 hour, nonstop flight to Dubai in the United Arab Emirates. I slept, I watched movies, I ate, all in my amazing support hose. (Unlike American carriers, Etihad's movies are free, and the food is good!) I hoped I didn't snore too much; it would be embarrassing to me and disturbing to my fellow passengers. It surprised me how quickly the time went by. I was excited, and stiff, when we arrived in Dubai. I signed onto the airport wi-fi so I could email my family and let them know I was safely on the ground.

But apparently, life didn't think I was quite humble enough. Just as I was thinking how smoothly the trip was going, it became complicated. The connecting flight was delayed. I spent another six hours hanging around the airport, wanting nothing more than to curl up on the floor and go to sleep. But that is unseemly in an Arabic country. Women are rarely out and about on their own, and traditionally it is extremely rude to show the soles of your feet, the lowest part of the body. So I pretended to have my wits about me and buried my nose in an electronic reader. Fortunately, I didn't need food since I'd filled up on the airplane. I wasn't ready to face currency conversion. I am terrible with numbers.

Finally, I boarded the plane to Kuwait City, a short hour and a half hop. I was definitely running on fumes at this point. My anxieties about being met at the airport skyrocketed – the plane was so late and there was that pesky lack of contact information. One good thing about fatigue is lack of energy; I just didn't have enough of it to get too worked up. I wondered again about the secret information experienced travelers have concerning passports, visas, and customs.

Walking into the airport, I drifted along with the other passengers from my flight in what I hoped was the right direction. It turns out I didn't have to know much because everyone has to go to the same place. I floated along in my own exhausted bubble, disconnected from the conversations gurgling around me. I was surrounded by men in long white *dishdashas* (robes) and women covered in black *abayas* (floor-length outer garments) a n d *hijabs* (head coverings). They had enormous amounts of luggage with them, some of it shrink-wrapped, some of it covered in little plastic raincoats with holes for the handles and wheels. Lots of expats, maybe Indian and Filipino, also milled around carting huge boxes with them. The sounds were a mixture of familiar airport noise and a cacophony of languages I barely recognized. I was in a daze of fatigue and visual and auditory overload.

Soon I saw reassuring signs in English and Arabic leading to passport control, which sounded like a good place to start. I wasn't sure if visa came before passport, passport before visa, so I just hoped for the best. We expats queued up at the line marked OTHER NATIONALITIES. Although I was exceedingly nervous about customs and the uniformed guards, it actually turned out to be pretty simple. No one asked me questions or searched my bags. I stumbled forward into a fenced off area surrounded by people holding signs as they waited to collect passengers, friends and families.

And there it was, *Alḥamdulillāh* (All praise is due to Allah), "Shamiya School" scrawled on a cardboard sign held by three friendly Arabic men. They didn't know much English, and I knew even less Arabic, but they helped me with my bags and boxes and got me to a car. It was hot! We drove about 20 minutes in the dark, attempting to converse. "Is brand new building," one of the men told me proudly. The darkness and my exhaustion interfered with making any observations of my own other than, *It is hot!*

We pulled up to one of the four apartment buildings the school uses for staff accommodations. The elevator took us to the fifth floor, my floor, and the friendly men ushered me into a one bedroom apartment. I was barely awake at this point and completely reliant on these gentlemen. I signed something; I didn't know what. The men departed with smiles, leaving me with 100 Kuwaiti Dinar which was worth about $350. I peeled off my very tired dress, and dropped into bed after about 24 hours of travel. I planned to sleep as long as humanly possible.

Chapter 7:

Ya Razzaq, The Supplier, The Provider

Our Power Grid

The next morning, a loud knock startled me out of deep sleep. What time is it? I was not expecting anyone; hell, I didn't even know anyone! The building was empty except for me; teaching staff came two weeks later than administrators. My heart pounding, I jumped out of bed, and pulled on the same tired dress from the day before. I opened the door to a woman dressed in long pants and a *hijab*. Speaking so rapidly I could barely keep up, she introduced herself as Nadine, the curriculum coordinator for Shamiya School. "We're going to align the curriculum this year," she enthused. That jolted me awake. Intellectual challenge is a double shot of espresso for me and curriculum alignment (ensuring academic subjects are taught in a coherent sequence in each grade level and across the K-12 spectrum) definitely fit the bill.

As she talked, Nadine took me out to get groceries and household items for the apartment. The full complement of linens we were told to expect turned out to be one flat sheet that didn't completely cover the bed. I had no way of knowing if contour sheets would even be available. The fully equipped kitchen had two plates, two bowls, two forks, two spoons, but no knives. (I wondered if the lack of knives was a holdover from traditional times. Bedouins [in Kuwait the word is *Bedoon,* or *Bidoon*] removed their curved knives from waistbands when they sat down to share a meal.)

So off we went to Lulu's Hypermarket (that's a real name) to supplement the fully equipped apartment. Lulu's is about the size of Costco, which I find completely overwhelming. But Lulu's is Costco with three floors. I was so dazed from lack of sleep that decision making was pretty much out of the question. Fortunately, Nadine was very happy to make all my decisions for me. And she knew all the insider information I needed to survive in the desert. For example, you have to take a cooler in the car with you when you shop in the summer or your eggs will be hard-boiled when you get home. Really.

To my delight, Nadine called Barb, the principal of the Special Needs Department, and we met for lunch. We drove to my first Kuwaiti mall, where we found a table in a French bistro complete with baguettes and beautiful pastries. Barb, it turned out, was from North Dakota. She was pretty quiet, but Nadine and I continued to talk shop. Nadine came from Salem, Massachusetts. Years earlier she had converted to Islam and moved to the Middle East. I was eager to hear more about how she had come to convert, and see if she knew anything about Sufism. But I decided to proceed slowly; I still had no idea if questions would generate tensions around Shia and Sunni differences.

When we returned to the apartment, Nadine

continued to make decisions for me, telling me how to arrange my furniture. "The couch can't go there; it's in front of the intercom people use to call when they visit." I was less grateful for this help; I am intolerant of intolerance to the fact that there are many paths to the same place; or the intercom. That intercom didn't ring once the whole time I was there.

It was still unbearably hot inside even though I had turned on the air conditioning the night before. I was seriously concerned about my ability to adjust. Nadine had been in Kuwait for about 20 years and knew the drill. "No, no," she said, "the air conditioning is not working at all." Oh, thank God, it can get better. She summoned Wahab, one of the men who brought me home from the airport, and after another six hours or so I had air conditioning. Phew! (Nadine might be a touch overbearing, but she knew her way around Kuwait.)

Oh, but wait … the power went out. Plunged back into unbelievable heat. This continued for the next week and a half until all the teachers from overseas arrived. Then power became more reliable.

I soon discovered I was not the only occupant of the building; the *haris*, a live-in guard/janitor, was living on the first floor. Unfortunately, he didn't know any English. I had tried to learn Arabic online; it seemed the respectful thing to do. It was so complex, however, I failed miserably. The Arab speakers couldn't seem to understand him either; apparently he was speaking an obscure rural dialect from Egypt. Imagine the quality of our communication. I was surprised to hear negative comments about Egyptians from two staff members who tried to help me communicate with him … I wasn't sure what to make of that.

On my second night, the *haris* knocked on my door, barged in uninvited, and proceeded to wash the bathroom floor and take out the garbage. Washing floors was easy in Kuwait; the bathroom and kitchen floors have drains in them, so you just spray them down and use a squeegee to sweep the water into the drain. I watched in horror as this man took my one towel (from my full supply of linens) and dried the floor with it. *That gives me a reason to figure out the washing machine.* Of course I had no clue how to respond to the work the *haris* did. I didn't want or need him to do any of that. I didn't think I was supposed to tip him, but I didn't really know.

The next evening, the *haris* knocked at my door again. I didn't open the door wide to welcome him, since his behavior had been weird and unwelcome the night before. He pushed his way past me and headed straight for my bedroom, fluffing up pillows and generally taking over my space. That is crossing the line, especially in a culture that does not allow men and women who aren't related to socialize together. Especially in the bedroom! I indicated sternly, using gestures and tone, that he needed to leave right now. He stopped bothering me after that, although I did have to stop smiling at him.

The apartment buildings that were used for staff housing looked like Soviet style blocks. I was prepared for this; a current staff member had posted a photo during the summer. Description, not complaint (although it might evolve into a complaint): the apartments were in a construction zone. Large trucks worked noisily into the night, as it was much too hot to work during the day. Piles of dirt were constantly moved from one location to another, for no apparent reason. Water trucks carrying desalinated seawater came around at all times of the day and night. There was no system of water lines; instead, water was pumped into storage tanks up on the roofs of buildings. Every night the loud, whining sound of the pumps interrupted my sleep.

Electricity was provided by generators located in the backs of semitrucks parked outside. The first couple of days they were frequently out of commission, which meant no AC. That was tough! The temperature was typically 118 degrees, and don't say, it's a dry heat. With humidity blowing off the Persian Gulf, the weather was often humid. When I finally got almost a full day of power, I was much happier.

The workmanship in our apartments was cheap and shoddy. Towel bars fell out of the walls, and the preferred fix was to stuff the holes left behind with toilet paper. I'm fairly handy, but these holes were too big to repair; spackle fell into the openings in the center of the cement blocks. The furniture was rickety, uncomfortable and shit-brown, and the bed, hard as a rock. As an old fogey, the lack of comfort was hard on my body, and I began waking up in pain every morning.

There were advantages to being in the desert. Because the water tanks were on the roof in the sun, instant hot water poured from the taps. I wouldn't have to turn on the hot water heater until around January; I just had to be careful not to get burned in the meantime. Another perk: the apartment was very sunny, which certainly suited this Seasonal Affect Disordered soul. Amidst the hard environment of Kuwait, I ferreted out the positives.

Chapter 8
Ya Muhsi, The Appraiser

The Mosque

I had arrived in Kuwait during Ramadan, a month of fasting to commemorate Muhammad receiving the Qur'an. Ramadan is followed by Eid-al-Fitr, three days of celebrating the breaking of the fast. As a result, there weren't many people around, especially during daylight hours when eating and drinking is prohibited. In fact, Kuwait remained pretty empty through September, because anyone who can afford to travels to cooler climes in the summer.

Initially, I didn't venture out much on my own; it was way too hot to be traipsing around outdoors, and I was pretty overwhelmed. I did manage to get to the corner store and the folks were really friendly. The shop was below the last apartment building in our row. It was the size of a large closet and crammed floor to ceiling with goods. Usually three or four people were working there, even though I could barely fit into the place by myself. It was a far cry from Lulu's.

I didn't understand the money yet, but the kind shopkeeps were scrupulously honest and helped me out. I had to wait a couple of weeks to get a bank account; these arrangements all go through employers, and I soon learned that anything bureaucratic takes an enormous amount of time in Kuwait. Way more than in the U.S.; think Vogons from *The Hitchhikers' Guide to the Galaxy*.

In the meantime, I bought milk using some of the Kuwaiti Dinars I received the night I arrived. What a rude shock when I poured it onto my cereal; it came out all thick and lumpy. Turned out that kefir came in a bottle identical to the milk bottle. I was utterly dismayed by this yogurt masquerading as milk, although after the initial shock, I came to prefer it.

The apartments were right next to a highway which was clogged with traffic at all hours of the day and night. My friend, Ilma who got a job in Qatar, Skyped me with a warning about a road in Kuwait. It was the third most dangerous in the world, based on number of fatalities. It was the road outside my window; the road I took back and forth to work everyday; the road where I saw a corpse on the way to work. (I didn't tell anybody at home about that; no need to worry them.)

Across this deadly highway was the most beautiful mosque. It had two golden onion domes and a golden minaret that caught the sunset every evening. At night it was lit by white light, a sign that it was a Shia mosque, according to my taxi driver. It broadcast the daily calls to prayer and every Saturday I heard ministry coming over loudspeakers in Arabic. The voices were loud and fervent, unlike anything I would have associated with religion in the U.S.

Out my window was a large flat area; a dry wasteland with no vegetation, nothing to hold the sand in place. Every evening a group of 20 to 30 young men gathered to play cricket. My internet connection wasn't working yet, so I couldn't google cricket, but it looked as if the players ran back and forth between two bases. Some days the young men were out of luck as the construction workers dumped mountains of sand over the cricket pitch. Undeterred, the teams moved their field to an adjoining, empty sandlot.

I hadn't seen the school or the nice parts of town yet, but that would come. I didn't have much to do; I must have left my Kindle on the plane because I couldn't find it anywhere. Maybe it was wise to simply rest, although I felt pretty good considering the length of the airplane flight. I began learning how to ask for help, no small achievement for someone as pathologically independent as myself. But there really was no choice, as I could do absolutely nothing outside of the apartment by myself.

Finally, the teachers began to arrive, in droves. Three nice young women moved onto my floor, two from South Africa and a gentle soul from the Bronx. She loved teaching in the Bronx; I admired her attitude.

I ventured out for a walk as I began to adjust to the heat. My young Bronx neighbor inspired me with her fearless exploration. Plus there was this constant need for food that forced me out of the house. I walked a few blocks to the store where all the construction workers and taxi drivers shopped. It was always hard to find a good path to the store because loose sand was everywhere, covering the walkways and roads alike. It was like walking on hot, dry sand above the high tide line. The sand slipped into my sandals, burning my feet.

Roads and pathways changed position daily as the sands shifted or trucks moved it around.

This store was about the size of a convenience mart in the United States. It was filled with spices and vegetables from India. Bean pods a good two feet long were stacked beside gourds covered all over with small bumps. I found what I learned later were *moringa* or drumsticks, that looked like celery. I experimented with many of them, figuring I could saute or steam just about anything. (It hadn't occurred to me to just ask what the vegetables were and look up recipes on the internet; I was still too independent.) They also sold ice cream and chocolate, those oh, so important staple foods.

I was usually the only woman in the store aside from the cashier, and she and I formed a bond of solidarity instantly. She always cashed me out before the men, which made me uncomfortable, but didn't seem to bother the men waiting in line. She was quick and capable, but cashiering was the only job she could get in Kuwait, even with a college degree. In the Philippines, there had been no jobs at all.

Other vagaries of life in Kuwait … all the drains in the apartment were covered with solid stainless steel disks. When I was done using the sink or shower, I covered the drain again; otherwise little lizards came up looking for water. I never found any; maybe they got off on a lower floor. I was told I didn't have to worry about scorpions, which was nice, but cockroaches abounded. Because there was no continuous water supply, I could easily run out halfway through a shower. What was I to do with a head full of shampoo and no rinse water? It was all kind of primitive for such a fabulously wealthy city.

Learning to dress for the culture was not as challenging as people often think. Westerners are not expected to cover themselves. Skirts with hems at or below the knee and pants are perfectly acceptable. (The Arabic women also wore pants and skirts, although this decision was heavily influenced by the men in their families.) While women cannot expose their entire arm, short-sleeved shirts were fine, and really, no one wants to see my upper arms anyway. Arabs do not seem to expose their arms at all, but I couldn't bear the heat with long sleeves.

Some of the women dressed in tight jeans and provocative tops, but they wore long sleeve jerseys underneath. They showed off their bodies, but without skin. The style is similar to what a Mormon woman might wear in the U.S. I did not see exposed cleavage and bra straps out in public, although I did in private homes. My personal clothing rules revolve around comfort. Modesty is just all right with me, and I didn't feel particularly restricted.

Kuwait is not as restrictive as Saudi Arabia. Most women in Kuwait go out to the mall or restaurants with female friends or family, and they do not have to be accompanied by a man. I was completely comfortable exploring by myself; it was safe and not too scandalous since I am a crazy Westerner.

The unannounced visits from Nadine became fewer and farther between. She was distracted by the new staff coming in, which afforded me a much-needed quiet day. While I was grateful for her help, she was intense, and I didn't want to be her personal project. Additionally, I'm accustomed to a lot more solitude than most, so her constant attention (and direction) was too much for me. In the wake of a peaceful day, I slept fourteen hours, which is a lot even for me.

I wondered if the big sleep was my body's reaction to the sand storm we had within days of my arrival. It was less ferocious than I imagined... not like the biting sand blowing painfully against my legs on a Maine beach. But extremely invasive, nonetheless. My glasses were in their case which was in my purse, but still they were covered in sand. I had only been outside for five minutes. It felt as though I was breathing sand, which I guess I was. I worried about it getting in my ears which are vulnerable due to the tubes penetrating my eardrums. So much sand infiltrated the apartment that it became clear I'd have to cover my computer. Its new home was inside a pillow case, which was almost adequate. And I had to clean more often; damn!

More likely though, the long sleep was simply jet lag; I'd been feeling fine, but am told that it catches up to you at odd moments. I have to say I enjoyed the luxury of that sleep which put a temporary halt to the unfamiliar and over-stimulating input from this very foreign country. The luxury of time was offset, however, by the hardness of the mattress, which left me with painful shoulders and hips each morning.

But I needed to get over that because the next day I would leave for work at 6 a.m., on the world's most dangerous highway, for new staff orientation. We had a week to get ready for students, which was good because a lot of the special needs classrooms were in a new building on campus, which was not yet finished. (Some things are the same the world over.) Also, supplies were squirreled away in locked rooms all across the enormous campus. There would probably be a lot of drama around getting people into classrooms. Drama seemed to be highly prized by Arabs and expats alike. I planned to avoid all that.

Chapter 9

Ya Wali, The Sole Governor, The Friendly Lord

Mural Outside the Shamiya Pool

I was anxious to start work. I'm not fond of sitting around waiting, and I tend to develop friendships with people I work with. The first real day at Shamiya School was exciting. We newbies gathered in the auditorium for staff orientation. The space stank of cat urine. Feral cats roamed everywhere, coming out at school mostly at night. I assumed the smell was the result of a summer invasion that would fade as human occupation drove the cats out.

An enormous information download about procedures and cultural taboos filled the first couple of days. Don't pick up anything with your feet. Don't disrespect the Qur'an. One teacher was fired because he pushed a backpack out of the aisle with his foot, and it turned out a copy of the Qur'an was inside. Don't use nicknames with students. Don't stand students outside the classroom for discipline. I wanted to be as respectful as possible and appreciated the advice.

Mr. Khaled, the superintendent, told us that he hoped we would be satisfied with our living arrangements, and eager to stay past our one year contracts. So if there was anything we needed, we should let him know. People mentioned the lack of linens and kitchenware. "We'll make that right for you," he responded. That sounded accommodating.

We were also admonished to watch out for people with "bad attitudes." Stay away from negativity. Don't say negative things about the school. Be careful who you trust or you might get stabbed in the back. A curious welcome-to-a-new-school speech. I didn't pay too much attention to any of this; my default is to expect the best of people. And, of course, my Avoid-High-Drama plan was firmly in place. Dodge all workplace gossip and politics, that's my motto. But, wow, are schools political places to work.

Shamiya School was a like a walled feudal village ... or a rabbit warren. I explored the campus in the steaming heat, finding all the buildings made of cement block and corrugated metal. Wood is an extremely rare and valuable commodity in the desert, and only used in elite homes and offices, like the superintendent's. Elsewhere, paint was peeling off the walls, and garbage was strewn all over. Doors didn't open and close fully. It made for a pretty stark physical environment. I thought back to the beautiful brochures I had seen of other international schools; no corrugated metal there. Frankly, I was surprised that wealthy parents would tolerate this for their children.

Most of the six campus buildings were two stories high with narrow stairways that could barely accommodate two people abreast. Not a great design for passing times in a school. The large Astroturf soccer field, where the Barcelona club provided football clinics for students, was a source of great pride. Did you know you have to water Astroturf, at least in the desert? I laughed so hard the first time I saw that, but then had to eat my words. Without watering, the temperature of the playing field skyrockets, an obvious problem for athletes. Watering also keeps the playing field level (I've never used that phrase literally before) and thereby reduces injury. But to be clear, it was a shopkeeper watering his four by six Astroturf carpet in the sand in front of his shop that I happened to see. I never saw our field being watered; maybe it happened at night?

Near the stores that housed our office supplies, I stumbled across one tiny, precious patch of real grass – a miniature oasis. I walked through the three outdoor play areas covered with spongy foam tiles, the only foot-friendly surface anywhere in the entire school. The school pool welcomed swimmers with a whimsical undersea mural; one of the fish was threatening to cut the airline of a very white deep sea diver, who has a look of horror on his face. I guess you had to be there.

One of the nicest buildings on campus was the school library. Its open design with lots of light, created a cool, quiet haven. Books are censored by the government in Kuwait, to remove any references to Jews, pigs, sex or even romantic love. The sense of peace in the building was counter-balanced by the knowledge that information and ideas were carefully controlled.

Two old classrooms up on the second floor served as the school's mosque. Practicing Muslims are called to prayer five times a day. Sometimes employees used this prayer room or they might unroll a prayer rug in their classrooms. They resumed their duties with calluses on their foreheads, reminders of their prostration in surrender to God. Several times a week the Arabic Department helped students to perform the proper ablutions before taking them into the classroom/mosque. I had images of a quiet, peaceful moment carved out of the tumultuous life of a school. Ironically, the students' mosque was one of the most raucous locations on campus. The kids were throwing shoes, hollering, and creating mayhem, as kids will do.

The Special Needs Department secretary arrived; what a blessing. Fayrah, who was from Egypt, knew how to get things done and gave me a lot of useful advice. Most importantly, she procured an office for me in the same building as the principal. The room initially assigned to me was in a different building, had no windows and was tiled like a bathroom. I was grateful for my tiny window and the proximity to Barb, the principal.

Beginnings can be difficult. Think of all the frustrations associated with the start-up of any new project. Now multiply that by 100. Seriously. In Kuwait, I couldn't even go pick up my own paper for the classroom or office. I had to fill out a request form, get a signature from another administrator, wait until Tuesday, which was the day our department could go to the "store," and then the storekeep doled out about a quarter of an inch of copy paper. I needed a ream. The same arduous process applied to getting copies made. There was only one copy center for this sprawling school of 2,500 students. Ironically, it was run by the twin brother of the storekeep who rationed the quarter inch piles of paper.

I was stunned by the amount of control and lack of trust in the school. We had to punch in and out of work everyday. Now that made me feel professional! Actually, that's not accurate. The time clock had been replaced with fingerprint technology to thwart people who might punch out for friends. We didn't have computers for students, but by God we had the technology to police our staff. Each of us gave the school the finger faithfully two times a day. Once everyone was inside the building, the gates were locked and staff were not allowed to leave, even to go across the street for a coffee.

Well, some of us couldn't go out; others left daily. I was not allowed out even though I was an administrator; I could discover no discernible pattern in who was granted freedom and who was denied. I soon learned it was a matter of *wasta*, who had pull and influence. *Wasta* was omnipresent in all interactions in Kuwait, but mysterious to an outsider like me. Although one thing was clear: I had no *wasta*.

Another mystery to me at school was the bulletin boards. Each of us, including administrators, had our assigned bulletin boards. We were required to change them quarterly, and staffers turned them into intricate displays of their own craft skills. This particularly annoyed me, because I don't give a hoot about bulletin boards. If I put anything on display, it is children's work that has not been prettied up, never adult-made works of art. I would much rather people spent their energy on great lesson planning. But at Shamiya School, people got into serious trouble for not taking good care of assigned bulletin boards. Especially people without *wasta*. I began to doubt my ability to avoid high drama.

We were expected to dress smartly at work; as

my friends can tell you, I much prefer to dress un-intelligently. In deference to the culture, I dutifully ironed my clothes (no dryer, so they always needed it). My usual response to the word iron is, "What is that?" We may not have been given bedsheets, but everyone had an iron and an ironing board. Several times a week the iron sputtered water all over my "smart clothes."

Wait, I think I'm having an epiphany … I'm gonna lay down my ironing board, down by the pile of sand, down by the pile of sand, down by the pile of sand, I'm gonna lay down my ironing board, down by the pile of sand, gonna iron clothes no more. (Sing it with me!)

It was obvious: I didn't want to do this ever again. I checked out the cleaners downstairs in our dusty little square.

Chapter 10
Ya Batin, The Hidden

My Office at Shamiya School

Finally the day came when the entire staff, not just the newbies, gathered at school. Except for the ones that didn't; a significant portion of our staff was not in the country for the first day. They had been hired, but the administration hadn't completed their paperwork in time for them to arrive for the start of classes. I was beginning to get a sense of the lack of efficiency with which the school was run.

Special Needs had its first chance to meet as a department. There were about 60 staff members, half of whom were Arabic and half of whom were native English speakers, serving 200 students grades K-12, all of whom were significantly intellectually disabled.

Wait? What? Are you sure? The superintendent told me we would be working with the full range of disabilities from mild to severe. I was not the only one who received this information; many of the new

61

teachers had been told the same thing at their interviews. When I mentioned the discrepancy to Mr. Khaled, he replied, "Well, at least you're not in a classroom." While not comforting, this was true; I would have been furious if I were in the classroom. I knew working with this population was not my strong suit, and had deliberately stayed away from it during my career. I deeply respect those who do it, but my calling has always been those sassy little boys that drive everybody else crazy.

There we all were, halfway across the world, with a superintendent who lied to us about who our students would be. Oh, and that bit about not admitting students with behavior problems – also not true. This did not bode well for a healthy work environment, but what could we do? We had left our jobs and were now knee-deep in a year-long commitment. Clearly there was no fixing the situation, so we settled in, with varying degrees of grace, to make the best of it.

To make matters worse, our first staff meeting was a complete debacle. My hope that we could at least run a clean shop in our own department was shattered. Barb repeated the same items over and over again. Staff members asked the same questions over and over again. People came up to Barb mid-sentence to ask quiet, individual questions over and over again. Creating a drama-free zone would be more difficult than I had anticipated.

It was at that first meeting I realized we had two sub-staffs, each with differing needs. The western staff understood pedagogy, but was lost without appropriate materials. The Arabic staff (Syrian, Lebanese, Egyptian, Jordanian) understood the cultural context, but had not been supported to learn best practices. Somehow, we would need to meld these two sub-sets into one coherent staff.

The challenges facing us were legion. Three new floors were added to one of the buildings on campus to deal with Shamiya School's increasing student enrollment. The construction of these floors was not complete. Originally the rest of the campus was to open on time and we would delay just those classrooms for two weeks. One day before classes were to begin, however, the decision came down to delay the start for the entire school. *Ah,* I thought in my black heart, *time for staff development.*

Barb and I sat down to talk about plans for this extra two weeks of Manna from Heaven. Even in the U.S., schools provide less training to their staff than my daughter received when she started scooping ice cream at the local shop. Two weeks was an absolute boon. Barb didn't have very many ideas; Angella, the counselor, and I had tons. I went home and drew up a tentative plan of training opportunities, based only on our best guesses about what the staff might need or want to learn.

We designed a nice program of team building, behavior management, assessment, attendance and paperwork requirements, none of which had been standardized in the past. Somehow, very little got done; every day, something came up. "I don't think we should do that," Barb would say, "we need to distribute books." This was a real concern ... the school ordered huge numbers of textbooks and workbooks that needed to get into the hands of teachers. No hands-on materials, no real books to read, no science equipment.

Using textbooks, especially with low-functioning

students, is an extremely outdated technique. State-of-the-art teaching involves inquiry-based learning, authentic reading tasks, hands-on materials, especially for math and science. I have not used a textbook in teaching since, well, ever. The western staff members and I were dismayed. Our image of international schools was that they were academically rigorous, using programs such as International Baccalaureate. IB programs emphasize hands-on learning. How would we teach?

We'd hand out all those textbooks, that's how. Did we really need 60 people to spend two weeks distributing books? Apparently so – teachers certainly were not going to be trusted to pick up their own materials – not with the level of control so evident throughout the school. Day after day staff development was put aside for book distribution. As time went by I learned just how much the Arabic teachers could squeeze out of those textbooks. Mr. Khaled filled me in on the years of absent leadership in the Special Needs Department. It was the Arabic staff members who maintained a welcoming learning space for students throughout the turmoil.

We managed to do a little bit of staff development; I used some adventure-based activities to begin building teams within the staff, and uncover some of the issues we needed to tackle. The first was a simple activity called a group juggle. The task was to get a series of yarn balls into the hands of every staff member once and only once in an efficient manner. We set goals, timed ourselves and crafted analogies between the group juggle and the work before us. Invariably the tension between efficiency and artistry is revealed by this simple activity. Such experiential initiatives surface issues more directly, and with a lot more fun and humor, than traditional professional development.

What became obvious immediately was the depth of love the Arabic staff members held for their students. At the same time, they were unconsciously limiting how much the kids could grow through low expectations and lack of appropriate materials and training. I filed away a mental note for future workshops on adjusting instruction to reflect interesting curriculum accessible to lower developmental levels. The western staff members were anxious to learn the cultural expectations of their new home and guide their students to the highest possible level of functioning. I would look for a collaborator from the Arabic staff to help us navigate the cultural waters.

Angella introduced behavior management techniques to our staff, some of whom had never used any kind of systematic approach to students not following directions, refusing to work, or hitting. Even though incidents occurred daily, there had never been any system of consequences for extreme student misbehavior. Individual teachers didn't have positive incentive programs to honor the students who did follow rules and work hard. The most rudimentary supports were completely missing.

And there were problems ... some of our students could not speak Arabic, let alone English, the exclusive language of instruction. Sometimes kids studied the difference between living and non-living things for 12 years in a row. Seldom was learning related to real life in any way. Twelfth grade students were still valiantly trying to master the sounds of the English alphabet without understanding sounds could be combined to make words. No life skills program existed to teach independence in daily living and work skills. There was clearly a lot to be done.

Chapter 11
Ya Hakam, The Judge

The Toy Store

When I start a new job, I observe for a while, learning the organizational structure, and figuring out the cast of characters. After being in Kuwait for three weeks, the time had come to do more than observe. This made life a lot more challenging; now I had to deal with my dismay and lack of experience with the rigid hierarchy that surrounded me. And figure out a way to respond that had integrity, but could blend with the new environment I was learning.

Shamiya School billed itself as international, as in having students from all over the world. In reality, all the students were Kuwaiti. It had an international staff and a large staff of Arabic speakers, but not so many Kuwaitis. There is a quota for the number of nationals who must be hired in Kuwait, but it is difficult to meet that quota. While the other Arabic staff members typically worked hard, some of the Kuwaitis didn't show up at all. We couldn't fire them because then we

67

wouldn't meet our national quota. The result was teachers with no teacher assistant all year, which meant no bathroom break, no planning time, no back-up when student behaviors flared; it meant teachers in unsustainable positions.

Academically, the school was in poor shape due to a long series of disastrous and corrupt superintendents. Among other things, previous administrators sold grades and class placements to their friends, Mr. Khaled told me. He had been superintendent for only one year.

I managed to get in trouble with Mr. Khaled right away, and was thereby introduced to a whole new cast of characters. In the orientation meeting, he said he wanted us to be happy and that he would take care of items that were lacking in our apartments. I thought he meant that, and turned in receipts for the basic items I bought. That's the process in every school I'd ever worked in. I didn't turn in a receipt for the microwave, that's not a basic, but a pot and a pan, yes. The result – drama. My phone rang. "Mr. Khaled needs to see you immediately," his very nice secretary told me. I dropped everything.

The superintendent's office was formal, reflecting his power in the organization. An enormous wooden desk dominated the room. A large picture of the Emir of Kuwait peered solemnly down from the wall. A maid brought in thick Turkish coffee in intricately painted ceramic cups. His swank office offered no clue as to what he might want to discuss. There were two other men in the room.

"Take a seat," he told me, looking agitated. The only seat available was between the two men, one of whom I had never seen before. I felt hemmed in between them. "Did you turn in a receipt for kitchen items?" he grilled.

"Yes," I answered, unclear why this was an issue. "Remember when you told us at staff meeting that you would make things right in the apartments?" I asked naively.

"You had no authority to ask for reimbursement. I would never say such a thing." he roared. "I know myself, and I would never have said such a thing!" His voice became louder and his tone more accusatory.

I was stunned that this was an issue in any way. I thought handing in receipts was standard operating procedure, although I probably should have known better after receiving my quarter inch of copy paper.

"Perhaps I misunderstood," I said, wondering why the other men were flanking me. One was the director of technology, who might have been delighted to see me rebuked. I hadn't been cooperative when he tried to take Special Needs furniture out of the Special Needs Department. I couldn't even imagine who the other man might be.

We repeated our litanies, "I never would have said that!"

"Perhaps I misunderstood." Over and over.

Finally, the man I could not identify announced, "It sounds like a misunderstanding." End of turmoil.

The setting for this conversation was designed to control and intimidate me; and perhaps allow Mr. Khaled to save face. Maybe the mystery man was a member of the School Board. Maintaining honor is paramount in Kuwaiti culture and is achieved through conflict. Nonetheless, I did not like the assumption that I was lying, or trying to put one over on the superintendent. I found it disrespectful, and completely unnecessary. And I could not figure out why people who were completely uninvolved in the incident were there to witness Mr. Khaled's attack.

This was the first situation I'd been directly involved with that highlighted cultural differences. I had observed similar displays on numerous occasions, but with other people as the protagonists. The western part of me (and the raging recovering codependent part of me) said, *You don't want to be in a situation which treats you poorly. That is one of the reasons you left the States.* The other part of me sagely observed, *This is not personal; some other issue is being worked out with me as the fall guy. Somehow, the superintendent needs to save face with other members of the school community.*

At home in my apartment, I read Stephen Batchelor. In his book, *Buddhism without Beliefs,* he noted that the Buddha did not conquer Mara (the devil, aka greed, hatred, persecution, anything that prevents entrance into the "stream of the path.") Instead, Buddha lived with Mara. The key being to view all the "negatives" we see in this imperfect world as transient; not to cling to and identify with them. In that context, I could take this incident as an unpleasantry that would flow downstream, passing me by. I didn't need to resolve anything, or do anything differently. I could simply proceed, and not take the conflict as criticism. I could live with the devil, not try to overcome him. So I decided to let the moment pass and stay in the now.

My perception of the control and intimidation in this incident was not paranoia or neurosis. In fact, everything was extremely hierarchical and micromanaged at the school. In the States, administrators say they value collaboration, involvement of all stakeholders, and creative thinking. At Shamiya School, decisions had to be approved directly by the superintendent; administrators (male or female) were not expected or allowed to take the initiative to work independently with their department staffs. The expectations of a professional were completely antithetical to what I had been expecting.

While much of this reflects a culture with a strict regimen guiding relationships, I suspect it was also due to the fact that the school is a for-profit organization. Even the superintendent had limited influence, his decisions being largely dictated by the Board. The goal of the Board of Directors was clear and all decisions were made with the financial bottom line in mind. Perhaps this accounted for the poor condition of the buildings, the lack of decent educational materials, and the blase attitude toward developing strong programs. These were discouraging realizations for my idealistic self. I heard that shattering noise again as more of my ideals crashed against the rock of truth.

The discouragement stemming from these realizations contrasted sharply with the joy I experienced as I got to know the staff members. I was excited at the connections they drew between the adventure team building activities and our work. The teachers were engaged and thinking and laughing. They actually asked to do more. I had never heard of a teaching staff asking for more staff meetings. I was so excited I set out in search of an old bicycle inner tube for adventure number two; a good excuse to go out exploring.

Not having a clue where to look for an inner

tube, I headed out into the dirt outside our apartments to hail a cab. The driver dropped me off at the nearest *souk* or market. The *souk* is no longer housed in tents, but in cement buildings. Yet, it retained the feel of the old *souks* with Bidoon women sitting on the ground surrounded by brilliantly colored cloths and head coverings to sell. I drank in that color as an antidote to the tans and browns of the desert. Little alleyways twisted and turned, hiding shop after shop of gold jewelry, white *dishdashas*, plastic *misbaha* (prayer beads), pots and pans, and every conceivable item a person might need or want. Throughout the area there were five-foot-high replicas of water urns with little cups hanging from hooks. Hydration is serious business in the desert heat, so water is available on every main street corner.

Because it is so blisteringly hot, all the stores close down during the heat of the day, and shopping is done in the evening. Miraculously, I stumbled across a toy store right away. It had inflatable camels and donkeys hanging from the ceiling. They were so ugly and easy to pack I thought I might have to get one for everyone I knew. But it turned out they cost thirty dollars apiece, too much for a gag gift. Anyway, I started trying to communicate what I needed to the shopkeeper who spoke only Arabic. It was definitely a challenge; even in the U.S., I can barely get people to understand why I need the strange items I use as adventure props. After much pointing and gesturing to the small bicycles, the shopkeeper found me an inner tube. He even gave me a discount, I think because I was nice to him and it was for kids; his young son was in the shop with him.

I was so pleased with my retail success that I

didn't watch where I was going. Loose paving stones and unexpected holes were everywhere; reinforcing iron stuck up in the middle of sidewalks. (I didn't yet know this would be common in most of the countries I visited.) I blithely stepped off the curb, onto a random, upended paving block. My ankle twisted as far as it could twist without breaking. I began an intense regimen of icing. The swelling wasn't too bad and I tried to take it easy, a challenging goal on Shamiya School's large campus. Not having a car also meant a lot of walking just to do the errands of everyday life amidst the sand and dirt piles.

Cutting back on walking afforded me downtime in which to process my experiences and observations. Surfaces in Kuwait were hard and uneven, the urban environment just as harsh as the natural one. Indoors was no better. Floors were concrete covered with fake marble-ish material. I missed walking on thick layers of pine needles outside and forgiving wooden flooring inside. Nothing was flexible or giving, literally or figuratively. Kuwait seemed a hard place.

Chapter 12

Ya Shahid, The Witness

How the Other Two Thirds Live

As I observed the culture surrounding me, a rigid hierarchical system emerged, with nation of origin being the initial sorting mechanism. The first question I was asked was always, "Where are you from?" (My brother advised me to tell people I was Canadian, but I never did.) The question surprised me; in the States I had learned that it is impolite, possibly insulting, to ask someone where they are from. Fayrah, our Egyptian secretary, asked if our black staff members were American or African. I assumed that African was bad from her point of view, though I never tested this assumption. And she is a delightful person who helped me enormously. I figure I'll be approaching grown-up status when I can wholeheartedly appreciate folks for who they are even when my own values are so affronted.

The divisions of status and opportunity begin with who is Kuwaiti and who is not. This turns out to be

74

a complicated question. Some people say they are Syrian, but they were born and raised in Kuwait, and have never set foot in Syria. In 1961, when Kuwait became independent from Britain,

> " ... about one-third of the population was given nationality on the basis of being 'founding fathers' of the new nation state, another third were naturalized as citizens, and the rest were considered to be *bidoon jinsiya* – or 'without nationality ... ,'"

according to *www.opensocietyfoundations.org*.

Because they are not considered nationals, they have no access to birth certificates, passports or IDs. They are not able to work, leave the country, or receive medical care; their children cannot attend public schools. Even if they graduate from private high schools, many are denied entrance to university.

> One Bidoon commented on the above website,
>
> ... My dad was a soldier and he fought
>
> in the war between iraq and kuwait,
>
> he is said to be Iraqi and that's
>
> why he cannot get a passport how is
>
> that true his parents and he and his
>
> grandparents lived in kuwait he and
>
> his brothers fought in the war trying
>
> to save their country one of them died
>
> and my dad got injured ... bidoons
>
> in kuwait can't get birth/marriage/death certificates they can't work can't drive

but still need to pay for health and education!!!

These are true women and men without a country.

Then there are the expatriates, now two-thirds of the population. In most cases, expats do the work. Manual labor is not valued by Kuwaitis, handy man skills not admired. Like me, the expats come looking for a doable job and a living wage. Unlike me, they were subject to a very narrow range of opportunities. Filipinas often worked in retail, but couldn't handle money in stores. Only one man was allowed to make change. Or a Filipina might work as a family's maid, taking care of children, shopping, cleaning and cooking. Indian or Sri Lankan males, if they were lucky, drove taxis; Indian or Sri Lankan females could work as maids, cleaning, supervising a bathroom or providing brute labor.

Many things that would be done with a forklift in the U.S. were done on the backs of expats in Kuwait. Construction workers labored under extremely hazardous conditions, pouring cement support columns, and then stacking blocks, leaving openings for windows. Nothing held the blocks in place. No hard hats were used, no harnesses when working at heights.

There was an abandoned toilet sitting by the site outside my apartment window. I had no idea where it came from, but it remained there all year. White tents were seen at every construction site, shelter from the sun being essential.

I worried over the construction practices in Kuwait. I built a house with my own hands in my younger days, so am fascinated with such things. The men worked on the building outside my apartment window from dawn until long after dark. The only source of light came from handheld flashlights. Spindly wood climbed up the side of the high rise, creating fragile spider webs of scaffolding. There were usually nine or ten cement trucks on site. They loaded up big funnels with concrete and the cranes lifted them 12 stories in the air. Then the funnel was tipped to pour the concrete into forms. One night as I watched it rise, I noticed a man standing on the edge of the funnel. He nonchalantly held onto the cable with one hand. 12 stories up. After dark. He was not roped in, he had no hard hat, he was just hanging out on the edge. Safety harness; I Don't Need No Stinking Safety Harness! Where is OSHA when you need them?

Indians had very little status in Kuwait, regardless of their level of education or expertise. One of our Indian teachers came asking advice for a family whose child had just been diagnosed with autism. The parents were devastated. But what was even worse was the fact that there was no school anywhere in the country that would take this child. If she were Kuwaiti, she would receive a free education, but that is only for nationals, not expats. When I was out walking one day, I came across the Indian school. At first, I thought it was a condemned building. Its windows were boarded up, the iron work on the railings rusty. Then I saw teachers leaving for the day. Not even a pretense of separate but equal here, and certainly no integration.

At Shamiya School, there was a large cadre of Indian and Sri Lankan women working as maids. They arrived every morning in beautiful saris, only to don shapeless, beige uniforms and be ordered around. It was very difficult to observe and not intervene. But this was not my culture. I had to observe the Prime Directive of non-interference with another civilization.

At first, I thought the maids at Shamiya had a pretty good deal, comparatively at least. I guessed they had some days off, unlike most other Indian, Sri Lankan or Bangladeshi workers. Later I learned they had to work weekends and holidays when the rest of the staff went home. The work was back-breaking and their living conditions cramped and confining. We teachers lived in the same neighborhood as the taxi drivers and construction workers, but we each had an apartment to ourselves. The taxi drivers were likely to have twelve people in their one bedroom apartment. They had left behind breathtakingly beautiful countries which they described wistfully. But there were no jobs there. So they took whatever work they were offered, their situations barely distinguishable from human trafficking. The young maids in families were particularly vulnerable. They had no freedom and were verbally abused by children and adults in public. Because the money and power is all in the hands of the Kuwaitis, there was seldom a way out of this indentured servitude.

Americans and Arabs alike treated the maids at Shamiya disrespectfully. I heard staff members hollering, "Maid, come here; do this." It was surreal. And at the same time, it reminded me of my country's living history of oppression. What would Martin Luther King, Jr. make of this?

Chapter 13
Ya Jami, The Uniter

Path to the Monastery, Largest Monument in Petra

Coming of age in Washington, D.C. during the 1950s and '60s, I had the privilege of being closer than most to the brilliant confusion of those changing times. During the Bay of Pigs Invasion, we figured that if the bombs did come, they would most certainly fall on the Capitol. My classmates and I crouched under our wooden desks for air raid drills, wondering even then how they would protect us from a nuclear attack.

My father worked as a political reporter for *The Washington Post*, covering the Nixon/Kennedy presidential campaign. Our family talked, ate, breathed politics during that heady time when anything seemed possible. My brothers and I freely roamed the halls of the Capitol building, welcome to sit in on Congressional sessions, and ride the subway to eat in the same cafeteria as Senators and Representatives. There were no badges, no security checks, not even any funny stares. Just free access to our own government.

Issues of race loomed large for me and many of my generation. My all-white, very affluent elementary school hired its first black teacher when I was in second grade. My mother told me about a friend of hers who asked her son how he liked his new teacher.

"I don't know," he replied. "She keeps sending in her maid." I was extremely aware of the issues of the time.

My father had a knack for knowing which events were truly historical as they happened. He made sure my brothers and I were in the crowd at the Lincoln Memorial for the March on Washington for Jobs and Freedom. I was ten years old, and it transformed my life.

That morning, Henry, John and I took a bus down to the Memorial. We found a place to stand under one of the trees closest to the foot of the steps. We ate our tuna sandwiches with potato chips where the lettuce should have been as the roadway between the Lincoln Memorial and the reflecting pool filled with people. Folks spilled out toward the Washington Monument. Soon a sea of bodies, 250,000 strong, of all colors, all ages, all genders, and all walks of life had gathered. We were there to support equality, freedom and opportunity for all people. "I have a Dream," King told us.

I wish I could describe that moment in a way that does it justice. But like any transcendent experience, it escapes words. There was a palpable intoxication of hope, love and purpose in that crowd. As the day grew hotter and the crowd grew larger, the mood brightened. People began wading in the Reflecting Pool. Never since have I been in such a crowd and felt safe and inspired.

We sang, "We Shall Overcome." I had tears running down my cheeks and chills running up my spine. And although Bob Dylan and Mahalia Jackson sang, I do not remember them at all. We celebrated the human spirit, and the American ideal of meritocracy. We felt the presence of God working through humankind, lovingly encouraging us to honor all, love all, respect all.

It is impossible to overstate the thrill of King's oratory. Fifty-one years later, my eyes still brim with tears and my heart with love. Whenever I am in D.C., I visit the tree I stood under on that day. I have taken my daughters to stand beneath its shade, hoping a little of that feeling remains for them to experience.

Three months later, John F. Kennedy was dead. Five years later, Martin Luther King, Jr. was dead. Washington, D.C., along with many other cities across the nation, went up in flames.

My civil rights education continued. My father was asked by *The New York Times* to write a story about one block in Washington that had been burned out during the riots/rebellion. He interviewed every business owner and every resident within that city block. And he took me along.

On a bright Saturday morning, we left the privilege of Chevy Chase, Maryland and drove into D.C. proper. Buildings in the inner city were still smoking and there was broken glass everywhere. We were there to interview a woman about her experiences during the rebellion. I was now fifteen years old and pretty cocky; I rejected the old Southern patina of politeness that accompanies growing up on the Mason-

Dixon line. I didn't say "Yes, ma'am" or "No, ma'am" to anybody. As we drove through the frightening remains of the rebellion, I worked on my bravado, my poise as a member of the *Different Clan*. I soon discovered that bravado didn't run very deep; I was completely out of my element and I knew it.

We arrived at the address for the interview, and opened the door to the tenement where our interviewee lived. It was dark as night inside, all the light bulbs in the hall burned out. My father and I carefully picked our way up three flights of stairs, stepping over the many missing treads. When we reached her apartment on the top floor, Mrs. Green graciously opened her home to us. She worked as a maid in houses near my own. She answered my questions with "Yes, ma'am" and "No, ma'am." I didn't think anyone should refer to me as ma'am; certainly not a dignified woman of 50 years. What I remember of our conversation is the gentleness of her spirit and words; her perseverance and steadiness in the most unsteady of times. My eyes were opened; I was introduced to a depth of injustice I had not truly understood before. Intellectually, I knew it existed, but now I had seen its human face. I wanted to make a difference, now and throughout my life, to break down the inequality between this fifty year old African-American mentor and myself.

The gift of these experiences was an understanding that how we treat each other is at the root of all joy and misery. If we can learn to treat each other with respect, dignity and appreciation, everything else will fall into place. We will not need a civil rights movement because we will treat all women and men with respect. We will not need an anti-war movement because we will treat all women and men with respect.

We will not need a feminist movement because we will treat all women and men with respect. We will not need an anti-poverty movement, or an environmental movement.

I knew my path. I wasn't there yet, but I knew which road I would be taking. I was strident in my youth and sure I knew the answers. I needed that surety in order to put one foot in front of the other. Only time would burnish off my rough edges and allow me to approximate Mrs. Green's gentleness of spirit.

Imagine bringing this history to Shamiya School where the Kuwaitis hate the Egyptians, the Sri Lankans think the Kuwaitis are lazy, and everybody feels superior to the Indians and Filipinos. I felt overcome with dismay when other nationalities were treated with disdain; when people's lives were cemented by the accident of birth. The word "maid," spoken by young African-American staff members, reverberated through the hallways without irony or self-consciousness.

It was a shaky tightrope to walk when the people I cared about and worked closely with every day were so easy with their insults. I found my values accosted at every turn. When I mentioned this to my friend, Eli, a Buddhist monk who very gently never cuts me any slack, he commented, "This sounds like the perfect situation in which to learn compassion and tolerance."

My way of coping felt too simplistic; I smiled at everyone and tried to learn names. A sullen young woman in our office transformed into a smiling, friendly human being. I gave clothes and personal warmth to a Sri Lankan worker with one blind eye. "Me love you," she said to me one day.

I hugged her, "I love you, too."

Is it enough? I've learned over time that I can't change the world, but I can do what's put in front of me. *Is it enough?*

When in another culture, it is not my right to challenge the norms. I am a visitor. Yet at the same time, I could not help but model my own values. In the past, I had thought of myself as a peace educator. I taught and practiced that if someone says something discriminatory and offensive, it is the onlookers' responsibility to speak up in defense of tolerance. Without that, there is a tacit approval of hatred. This is hard enough in my home culture, but it was quicksand in Kuwait. I never knew where the landmines were buried.

"Shatter your ideals upon the rock of truth," my Sufi teacher had told me. Even the ideals of human dignity and equality?

Chapter 14

Ya Mani, The Preventer

The Copy Center at Shamiya School

We were now a week away from the start of school. My frustration continued to mount, as Barb postponed more trainings to distribute books. If I stacked up all the assertive incidents in my life prior to arriving in Kuwait next to the assertive incidents in the first three weeks at Shamiya School, the school stack would tower over the U.S. pile. I was only asking for paper or copies, or to keep people from stealing our supplies. I was having a lot of trouble staying in the now; in fact, I was feeling some drama coming on.

Then, one of our teacher assistants mentioned in passing that our student assessment packets were not going to be run off. The copier guy, decided he wasn't going to copy them. He didn't inform me that he wasn't going to copy them. We couldn't plan for students unless we had assessment data to show their level of functioning. So I marched over to the metal shack that houses the copy center and pulled rank on the copy twin. "I like and respect you, but you don't know what the Special Needs Department requires and I do. Make those copies."

"It is a lot of copies, Madame. Too many."

"Let me say again, I know what our department needs to run well; make the copies."

"How many do you need, Madame, it is a lot of copies."

"I need the number of copies that is on the copy request form. And I need them by Sunday."

To make matters worse, another day went by with nothing to do. We were still waiting for the construction to be finished and the books to be handed out. Everyone gave the finger to the finger print machine to get paid, but there was nothing to do. Barb had taken no action on the staff development plan, just happily spent her days chatting with people. I hate asking people, or being asked myself, for that matter, to just put in time. Frustration piled upon frustration.

Barb called me at home asking where the staff development proposal was. She could never seem to find her own materials. I emailed her a copy and hoped against hope there would be something to do the next day. Perhaps the superintendent had given Barb her marching orders.

Barb called me at home again, asking me to finish up some work of hers that she hadn't completed. I was in the habit of regularly letting her know I was happy to help with administrative tasks. I wanted to be a good team member and pull my weight, and I do have a lot of experience to draw upon. Usually her answer was no, she didn't need any help. But on this occasion, she wanted me to finish scheduling the supervision duties at the various gates throughout the campus. It was an odious task, and I was off the clock.

One of the few boundaries I have ever been able to establish is to leave work at work. I'll work long hours when needed, but I support myself and everyone else in having a balanced life. I didn't take kindly to being asked to pick up the slack on a task she simply hadn't bothered with. "Oh, I'm so sorry, but I don't have the necessary information at home with me."

Next, a printer from Barb's office disappeared. At Shamiya School, technology was an endangered species and printers were rare commodities. Although the teachers had rafts of weekly paperwork to complete and submit as hard copy to the office, they had no access to a printer. Barb ordered a new printer which freed up the old one for other uses. Initially the plan was to put that printer in my office, but it made more sense to me to put it in the workroom for the teachers. A good administrator makes life easier for colleagues.

Best laid plans: when the new printer was installed the old one vanished. Where was it? Barb didn't know. Questions arose in my mind: *Is she aware of what happened to it? Why can't she track it down? Why doesn't she attempt to track it down? What does she do all day?*

All that stress and frustration bounced me right out of the now. I lost my center, and with it the sense that everything was fine at this moment in time. I blundered over into worry and projection, rational thought and disappointment in an irrational world.

The next few days Barb was out sick with an

upper respiratory infection. The Kuwaiti climate is murder on the respiratory tract and often induces asthma in previously healthy people. She called me at home to say that staff would not be responsible for any classes on Sunday, the first day for students. The format would be a meet and greet. This was news to me. "Are you sure?" I asked. "We just delayed school by two weeks. Who made this decision? Are you sure this is right?" I had a bad feeling.

"Yes, that's the plan," she assured me. "We decided on the meet and greet format at the Leadership Team Meeting. You need to announce this to everyone tomorrow."

I dutifully announced the meet and greet plan to the staff. By Thursday, the last day before the weekend, stress levels were through the roof. The different workweek alone, Sunday through Thursday, was enough to throw us Westerners off.

But the bad feeling persisted; it just didn't make sense. Finally I checked in with the elementary school principal who attends the same leadership meetings as Barb. It turned out, classes were to be held as usual on Sunday; no more delay, no meet and greet. At this point teachers had only half a day to prepare lessons for a full day of classes. I made the rounds to each classroom as quickly as I could to give staff the news. *How did this happen? Why is our department the only one that received this erroneous information? Is Barb confused? Defiant?*

Things were tough that Thursday. Fortunately, there was a weekend to decompress after the tensions of school. So I escaped. I went to see a movie (which was censored for bad language and sex scenes, which is actually OK with me), chatted with a friend, practiced yoga and meditation, all of which did me good.

The saddest thing happened that weekend; all those mounds of dirt moving onto the cricket pitch emptied out the foundation for a new apartment complex. The big hole in the big sand lot was becoming a big, tall building that would obliterate the sweet sight of the beautiful mosque.

I received news from back home about uproar in Kuwait; an anti-Islamic video had been created in the States. My friends were worried that the incident might result in demonstrations that could endanger me. I didn't even know about it. (To the utter dismay of the three members of my immediate family who have been journalists, I don't read the paper much. It's my way of dealing with the overload of sorrow in the world.) A couple of hundred people did demonstrate in Kuwait, but I did not see them or hear about it. Kuwait loves the small dramas of life, but is a pretty calm place overall.

The disrespect for another faith exemplified by that video is anathema to me. Devout Muslims have great respect for religious traditions that worship one deity. (Traditions with multiple deities are another matter.) My Sufi training intersects well with my desire to be respectful of different points of view. All religions, according to the Sufis, teach the same truth, the same Message. The idea of generating violent conflict over small differences in doctrine makes no sense to me. No God would want us fighting in His/Her name. As Jackson Browne sings, "I'm on the side of the rebel, Jesus."

Chapter 15

Ya Matin, The Firm

The Shifting Sands

After the weekend I felt back on an even keel, ready for the next round. Now I couldn't wait to see the school fill up with kids on Sunday.

Not everyone returned to school on Sunday, however; there was much dragging in a little bit at a time. Many Kuwaitis have so much money that they don't have to work, so it's hard to convince students or their parents that education is very important. Extending a vacation to avoid the heat is a much more practical value for them. Nonetheless, it was wonderful to watch our rabbit warren fill up with children, forgetting all the petty dramas and remembering what we were there for. Soon, the classrooms were running smoothly. We started with three staff members still out of the country, and many taking personal time during the first week, which would never happen in the U.S. We had perfect staff attendance during those weeks with nothing to do.

There were no substitutes so getting all those classrooms covered was difficult at best.

Although I tried to avoid it, creating the duty roster became one of my responsibilities. There were about 20 physical positions around the campus that were staffed before and after school and at lunch times to be sure students stayed in supervised areas. I had done the duty roster about seven times and still had some changes to make; sometimes because I wasn't given accurate information, and sometimes because I made mistakes as I always do with scheduling.

Now on the first day, I had to go around the entire campus, five buildings and 2,500 kids, to police the duties. Was everyone at their post? Did I have to call someone who forgot? There were no phones in classrooms so everyone had to rely on their own personal cell phones. It was frantic, and I have to say, policing is not my favorite role. In spite of all this patrolling, I still managed to visit all twenty-three special needs classrooms two or three times during the first week. That was satisfying.

The principal and I were called to a meeting with the superintendent. After my last visit with Mr. Khaled I was feeling less than confident.

Khaled immediately focused in on Barb. "Did you tell your staff there were no classes on Sunday." I don't know how he found out about this, but he definitely had his sources. Straight-faced, Barb told Mr. Khaled that she never mentioned a meet and greet. I was stunned! Never in my professional life, had I experienced such brazen self-interest trump any semblance of reality. After busting my chops cleaning up her mess, I was pissed and did not let her words go unchallenged.

"Actually, Barb, that is what you told the staff."

Truth telling is something I cannot seem to avoid, but this was certainly going to complicate my relationship with Barb. *How was I going to respond to flat-out lies? How would I relate to her in the aftermath of these lies? How should I conduct myself with Khaled?*

Clearly, I had found my way into A FOG, my friend, Mackenzie's, abbreviation for Another Fucking Opportunity for Growth. And this is how I cope with A FOG ... I turn on my low beams and search for some meaning, some learning I can wrestle from the situation. I try to find the cleanest, most compassionate way through that I can muster. I decided that I would be scrupulously fact-oriented. I would make no assumptions or attributions of motive in my remarks to Barb or Khaled, although in my black heart I was convinced Barb was deploying a not so covert Cover-Your-Ass operation.

After leaving the office, I remained cordial with Barb. As new incidents of less than accurate reporting occurred, I stated my observations; I wanted her to know I knew. Otherwise, she would happily throw me under the bus, and I had no intention of letting that happen. I continued to work hard with as much integrity as I could manage, collaborating with Barb as much as she would allow. I reminded myself that I had known from the get-go that this would either be my dream job or the job from hell – and that a lot of that rested with the principal.

On the brighter side, I was summoned to the Big Office to meet with Mr. Khaled alone. This was the first time he and I had talked privately since I was called on the carpet for turning in receipts for apartment supplies. He had come by my office earlier looking for Barb, appearing almost sheepish. I could have imagined that. When I arrived, he greeted me warmly, supporting my theory that last meeting's hollering was a face-saving gesture in front of the financial arm of the school. Or maybe he was just better at letting things pass than most people I know, including me.

Mr. Khaled told me he was hearing a lot of good things about the work I was doing, from staff, administration and even the Board of Directors. He wanted to know how things were going in the department. "Do you want tactful or honest?" I asked him.

"Honest."

Thank God. "I'm frustrated because there is no progress on any front. We got very little staff development done. There is so much misinformation floating around, that it is hard to operate. Our staff does not have access to printers and materials." The list went on.

Mr. Khaled already knew how bad things were. He went on to tell me that this department had been adrift for almost 10 years with corrupt or non-existent leadership and guidance. The lack of leadership was so extreme that Khaled split the special education programs for learning disabilities and vocational education off from the program for more seriously intellectually disabled. Normally these are all combined in one special education department. Since no one was managing the department, and a number of teachers were simply not teaching, it was too messy and unwieldy to keep everyone under one umbrella.

Mr. Khaled told me the school was planning a new building for the Special Needs Department the following year, and I got the feeling he really wanted to provide well for our students. He repeatedly urged me to confront Barb; I replied, "I always push, but at the end of the day, I am not her supervisor, only her colleague, and her subordinate colleague at that."

The plot thickened as I was called in a week later to meet with Mr. Khaled again. He informed me that his plan was to make me principal next year. *Imagine that. Oooh, how good that felt to hear. He had observed my work and heard good things from the other administrators. It was so easy for him to notice my* Differentness. *(Darn it, I can't get my swelled head through that doorway.)*

Now I had some thinking to do. I was still troubled by the incident of public humiliation over reimbursement in Khaled's office. If it was a one-time thing, no problem, everyone is allowed an off day here and there. If it is standard operating procedure, this was not the place for me. After a lifetime of abusive relationships and jobs that were exquisitely co-dependent, I was looking for a healthy situation for myself – one with a degree of respect and maybe even support. Such positions exist, I knew, because I had been lucky enough to work in two different organizations that exemplified these principles.

I also needed to consider my relationships with staff; I felt appreciated by those who wanted to see the program improve and I was pissing off the complainers. This is the nature of being an administrator because there is no way to please everyone. But I needed to be able to confront issues positively without being angry myself. This has never been my strong suit. I tend to tolerate problems until I've built up a good head of frustrational steam and then the confrontation comes boiling out. That's a recipe for hard feelings. I had a lot of work to do on the personal level. And the drama potential ... very high. I know, I'll make a scale like the national parks use to represent fire danger. "Drama Danger Very High. Extinguish All Combustible Materials."

You might think that was plenty of food for thought for one day. But you would be wrong. After school all the new staff trundled off to the Ministry of Social Affairs and Labour to be fingerprinted for our visas. Two busloads of tired, hot teachers headed over to a building that looked like a cross between the worst Department of Motor Vehicles Office and a seedy Greyhound station. There was a sandstorm and the AC was barely working. We waited there for three hours. My poor, twisted ankle was dangling in the air all that time, and this came on top of much pounding on concrete during the week. My ankle started to throb as my short legs dangled above the floor, but there was no way to elevate my leg and relieve the pressure.

The men and women had separate waiting rooms. Three times the men were marched out of the building without being fingerprinted. They had incensed one of the government workers by being too loud. (We *had* been told to be quiet.) It was a lot like the Soup Nazi episode of Seinfeld. You look cross-eyed and you are out!

This was also the night scheduled for us to go to the Aware Center, an organization promoting cultural understanding between Westerners and Middle

Easterners. So we piled back onto the bus (without the men because they were bad, and hadn't completed their fingerprinting) and headed over. Or tried to – our bus driver had no clue where it was, and of course, neither did we. We literally drove around in circles for at least an hour. Now we were really tired, hungry and thirsty; and cranky.

Finally, after many phone calls and failed routes, the driver found the place and parked. We entered a large, white building flanked by Corinthian columns, offsetting the traditionally Arabic arches above the windows. A satellite dish was nestled in a life-size plastic palm tree behind the locked gates that enclosed the building. We were ushered downstairs to a comfortable room with chairs and sofas lined up along each wall, *diwaniya* style. *Diwaniyas* are gathering places where men held business and social gatherings with male colleagues. As in many Kuwaiti homes, they feature divans arranged against each wall, leaving the middle of the room unobstructed.

A Kuwaiti man told a story of his culture shock when he went to the U.S. to study at a university in Texas. One hot day, he became riveted, he told us, by a girl's tight T-shirt and bouncing breasts. Before coming to the U.S., he had never socialized with any women outside his family. The girl, offended by his staring, demanded, "What are you looking at? You want to see them? Here!" whereupon she yanked up her T-shirt before bouncing away.

Although I knew it was culturally inappropriate to show the bottoms of my feet, I spent the rest of the evening with my sad, hurting foot up on a chair. Someone was kind enough to bring me a plate of food. It was fantastic! I ate and waited for the bus. All told, this was one crazy fourteen-hour-day.

I had plans for the weekend, but ended up tethered to the couch and a ziplock bag of ice. My ankle hurt more than when I was initially injured. I hoped my suspension system would get used to all these hard surfaces.

Chapter 16

Ya Sami, The Ever Listening

Kuwaiti Aesthetics

One of the many royal palaces was situated near Shamiya School. Kuwait is a constitutional monarchy, and a few members of the ruling Al Sabah family attended our classes. It was hard to determine the status of the palaces. The one by the school was surrounded by metal construction walls, and partially in ruins. Some of the palaces were going up, and some were coming down. Some were being preserved in an in-between state to remind people of the Iraqi invasion. Although, I did not hear one reference to the war the entire time I was in Kuwait.

There was a hospital across the street from the school with tree trunks displayed on the front lawn. In the Pacific Northwest, they would have been abandoned as slash. Only the most important buildings have any wood in them at all; the use of wood conveys status. Wood is often displayed like a work of art. After I began to travel, I noticed this throughout the Middle East.

Appreciating the preciousness of water is unavoidable in the desert. Although I've always been a good conservationist, in Kuwait I never left water running, or poured it down the sink. Instead I'd save it for cooking or brushing my teeth. The water in Kuwait comes from de-salinization plants so scarcity is not much of a problem; but still ...

Checking the weather in Kuwait is just as unnecessary as checking it in Washington State had been, but for opposite reasons. It's always cloudy and 50 degrees in Port Townsend; in Kuwait it's always sunny and 118. The first time I saw clouds in the sky was a red letter day!

Skin does not like the desert, hates the desert. When my hands started to split, I asked for advice. More asking, I was getting good at this. I started putting foot cream on my hands during the day and olive oil on them before bed. Sometimes I felt like a bad Italian meal, but it did work. The upside of all the sun was the enormous amount of light. I perked up like a flower after being in the clouds nine months of every year for the past 16.

The bathroom drill is quite different in Kuwait. It involves a little sprayer, like we would have at the kitchen sink, beside each toilet. Empty whichever organs need to be emptied, spray off and then use the thinnest possible toilet paper to dry off. But, and here's the tricky part, don't flush the toilet paper. Please visualize bucking 59 years of prior and opposite training to throw used toilet paper in the garbage. It was not easy. And why can the toilet flush solid waste but not the cheapest, flimsiest toilet paper ever? Clearly, I was an inexperienced traveler; this is routine in most places around the world.

The spraying off is a nice system especially when it's so hot. Might be a bit of a shock in the winter, though, in the absence of heating systems. There was a ubiquitous job throughout the country that I would not wish on anyone. A person is hired to sit all day in public bathrooms. Of course, this occurred in the States as well, maybe still does in luxury destinations. Poor women getting tips for handing people towels in the bathroom and worse.

Shamiya School's Kindergarten Principal used to say, "Kuwait is a nice place once you get used to the lack of aesthetic." The truth of this statement emerged when I went in search of some cheap lamps, and a footstool for the apartment. Everything in Kuwait is pink ... and tacky ... and glitzy. If the Kuwaitis had pink flamingos they would bedazzle them. And this is the expensive stuff. Did I mention the pink?

I needed to get rugs for the apartment, but didn't have enough cash for the taxi to the store. The dinars I had been given on arrival were just about gone and my bank account had still not been set up by the school. So it was time to exchange some of the American dollars I had brought with me. I trudged through the sand to the money exchange, but they didn't want my dollars. "Too many dollars. Want to sell. No take more dollars." Not an optimistic sign for the strength of the U.S. economy.

This presented a formidable problem; Kuwait is a cash economy. Outside of the big malls merchants rarely take plastic; I had no way to get to another money exchange. Fortunately, Nadine offered to pick me up and take me to an exchange in another area while she did her shopping. I hadn't seen her in quite some time, and I was grateful for her help.

The malls in Kuwait were enormous. When I was reading up on the country before I arrived, I read there were two things to do for recreation, eat and shop. I didn't believe that as I can almost always find something cheap to do. Unfortunately, it turned out to be true. One mall is several miles in length and has two Bath and Body Works stores, two Gap stores. Why? Because no one is likely to be willing or able to walk the entire length of the mall.

The grocery stores were also enormous. The one closest to the apartments, Lulu's, was three stories high. The shopping carts were equipped with magnetic wheels that clicked into place on wide, sloping escalators taking shoppers from floor to floor. Everything was available there, including a lot of expensive western food. All the food is imported as no crops could grow in the desert. The selection was quite overwhelming, especially for a Costco-phobic like me.

Lulu's was closer to the desert than the school. The closer to the desert, the more covered the women were. So in the midst of this modern shopping behemoth, women wore the *abaya* and *hijab,* and even black gloves. Then they pulled an iPhone out of their gargantuan designer purses. Kuwaiti culture is in such a state of transition.

There are many different kinds of coverings for women. Some wore a *nijab* which is a flap of black cloth covering the nose and mouth. I watched a woman eating soup out in public with a *nijab;* it was tricky. Some women wore complete head coverings with two eyeholes cut into them. Imagine the peripheral vision. Then they put their sunglasses on top of the head covering and drove. On the most dangerous highway in the world.

In the apartment, I found I took life at a slow pace more easily than I had in the States. I felt more detached, probably because I was not living in my own culture. This seemed to free me up to do as I pleased. In the States, I am always self-flagellating because I "should" have a better social support system. In Kuwait, I had the patience to allow myself to live at my own speed. Maybe I was finally growing up.

When I came to Kuwait, I had hoped to have an instant community, just add water, to shore up my shabby support network. However, most of the staff were very young, some just out of school. They liked to go out of an evening, and shop or smoke *sheesha*. (*Sheesha* is flavored tobacco smoked in hookahs. Many restaurants in Kuwait have gorgeous hookahs available and serve their customers for hours at a time.) Neither of those activities was my cup of tea. Actually, I don't like tea or coffee either. I really am handicapped in some of the social graces. It's especially difficult in this culture where the offer of tea or Turkish coffee is part and parcel of hospitality. I had to at least learn how to drink tea.

For the most part, I was content to hole up in my apartment at the end of the day and read or write. Writing became a necessity for me, a vital way to process all the new experiences, and I sent lengthy emails home every week or so. I worried I might burn out my friends with such long messages, but they were quite loyal. Ironically, in many ways I was in closer contact with friends than I had been when living in the

U.S.

I did occasionally need to get out of our dusty neighborhood. My physical surroundings affect me strongly; I need to have beauty around me. There wasn't any beauty in the neighborhood with the exception of the world-class sunsets I could see from the apartment. The air quality was awful due to blowing sand and high pollution. There was often a sulfur-y smell in the air, all of which made for good sunsets.

One day when I needed to escape I went to a movie at Imax, my first 3-D movie in Kuwait. Note the irony of viewing *To the Arctic* in 118 degree weather with high humidity. It actually felt refreshing. During the credits, names keep breaking up into chunks of ice that flew out at the audience. A bit assaultive, but cool.

Cool is a good feeling in all that hot, dry sand. And it's hard to come by in the desert. The desert seemed an inhospitable place to me. I had seen no wildlife so far, except for feral cats and dogs. No birds were flying around or taking dust baths, no squirrels or chipmunks. No native plants to speak of, really quite desolate.

In the apartments, I found several irreverent people to ride to school with. They were only 20 years younger than me. They were funny and filled me in on important information about the country.

For example, they told me about the very high rate of genetic disorders in Kuwait, including Down Syndrome, because of the prevalence of intermarriage and older mothers having children. I also suspect that the terrible quality of the environment and the aftermath of the war have a lot to do with the prevalence of disabilities. On top of that, being disabled remained a source of enormous shame. Think the United States in the 1950s when disabled kids were kept in their homes and didn't attend school. In Kuwait, they might not even be allowed to play with their non-disabled siblings in the same household. It's very sad.

Arab boys are allowed to do anything they want. I had read this in my cultural studies over the summer, but didn't believe it. As a member of the Sufi Order, I'm aware of anti-Muslim bias. I take such remarks with a grain of salt. But one of my carpool buddies said she was in the mall one day when a boy came up to her and hit her. Just randomly came up and hit her. She gave him The Look, she gave the parents The Look, but the parents didn't pay a bit of attention.

The parenting within these wealthy families mirrored the kind of neglect and disinterest that we sometimes see in families with lower socio-economic status in the States. They eat crummy, processed food and the rate of diabetes is off the charts. There simply is no motivation to learn or work. I was not sure how to go about creating a structured environment at school when it was the only place in kids' lives where anyone asked them to meet any kind of expectation.

After graduation from high school, a Kuwaiti teacher aide told me, Kuwaitis are guaranteed a job from the government. They receive a paycheck whether they show up for the job or not. After two years of marriage, the government supplies couples with the money to buy a house.

This leaves little motivation to work, but does create a n enormous sense of entitlement. (As a proponent of guaranteed income, I feel chagrined writing this.) Kuwaitis expected their *wasta* to give them access to the best merchandise, and a life of incomparable ease. I watched as they arrived late for boarding the airplane. While everyone else waited, they loaded shopping bag after shopping bag into the overhead bins. The notion of earning something did not enter into any conversation to which I was privy. Kuwaitis expected their children to receive A's whether they did any schoolwork or not; teachers who protested could be fired. Despite years of effort, my judgmentalism flared.

Chapter 17

Ya Afuw, The Forgiver

Oil Wells Off the Kuwaiti Coast

I had feelings about the Kuwaitis and their sense of entitlement, and they were all negative. What will they do when the oil runs out and they need to earn a living? How will they learn to work, have the discipline to show up on time, or develop pride in a job well done? My harsh opinions did not actually match reality. The Kuwaiti government established a sovereign wealth fund as early as 1953. The fund helps the country diversify its investments. Kuwait is also known for its extensive experience in financial-sector firms. The government was responding responsibly to this problem. But I was on a roll.

I also had negative feelings about Americans and their sense of entitlement. I knew more than a few who felt the world owed them. One friend contacted everyone he knew to contribute money toward a trip abroad he wanted to make. No one pays for my holidays. Another young friend always "needs" the chair that would best fit an elder in the room. I was quiet in my judgment about these things, but it was there. "What about hard work and earning what you have?" my righteous indignation snapped.

In fact, I was a captive of my indignation. Family and culture conditioned me to value hard work by individuals as opposed to society at large taking care of its citizens. In truth, when I thought carefully, I championed the idea of guaranteed income for all. But the message I absorbed from childhood on was that people succeed through hard work and sheer determination. Toward that end, I took on important, challenging jobs. I worked hard on the relationship with Ben. We worked hard together, and built a house with our own hands. Success was the result of my own efforts; I didn't ask for help from anybody.

But I wasn't succeeding. Leaving Ben was a wrenching decision that I avoided for an achingly long time. After all, a person is not just an alcoholic, and I loved him deeply. Ten years went by between my realization that alcoholism was destroying our lives and the moment I finally stepped out of the relationship. The universe provided many opportunities to find my way out, but I ignored them. I tried valiantly to fix what was, ultimately, unfixable. Giving up on the commitment I made to Ben felt like a failure, even as I knew this was the only healthy thing to do for my children and myself, and possibly for him.

My spiritual training taught me that the essence of the soul is joy. I thought that once I made the tough decision to get out from under the alcoholism, joy would emerge. While there was definitely a certain freedom to living in safety with my two girls, my melancholy persisted. I wasn't ducking God anymore, I was making decisions based on guidance. Where was my joy?

I plugged away to support the kids and myself. My compassion for the sole breadwinners of the world grew as I bowed under the pressure of providing for my family. Every time Lily or Addie needed a new pair of shoes, I panicked. We didn't have enough extra money to buy a pizza once in a while. I was exhausted all the time. I assumed it would get easier as I got used to being on my own. It didn't. I assumed that my reward for making the hard choices and doing the hard work was just around the corner. It wasn't.

Unwittingly, I had developed a formulaic view of life. When I was in elementary school, the teacher taught us the Golden Rule: "Do unto others as you would have them do unto you." I interpreted this as an equation. If I did the right thing, the right thing would be done unto me. If I did the right thing, I would be happy. I wasn't prepared for the bumps and bruises that buffet us all. I wasn't prepared for the lack of reciprocity that characterizes so many interactions. Reality left me confused and reeling. Where was my joy? I was entitled to joy!

This confusion played out in my work life as well. I expected to be appreciated for excellent work. Instead, administrators tend to reward the cranky, complaining employee, not the one who comes in everyday, and quietly, competently keeps the place going. If I hadn't grasped that lesson in the U.S., my time in Kuwait beat it into me. Any misunderstanding resulted in a full-blown confrontation complete with accusations and back-stabbing. Not much truth, however. The blow might land in the aftermath of doing exactly what the superintendent ordered. Or it might fall because of a personal relationship between a Westerner and a Kuwaiti outside of school. These eruptions exploded even if, perhaps especially if, the staff member involved was highly skilled.

In the clear light of the desert, with no barrier to the heavens, all this stood out in stark relief. My longings began to sound dangerously like a sense of entitlement. In fact, they sounded a lot like a child stamping her foot when she didn't get her way. I've always hated being told the people who annoyed me were just like me. Yet the Kuwaiti sense of entitlement opened the window to seeing my own.

Suddenly, I realized I was angry at God. God had not delivered on His "promise" of joy and happiness in my life. I had forgiven Ben, but I was still pissed off at God. I had earned the right to have a good life. I had sacrificed to pave the way to a happy life. What had gone wrong?

Feeling entitled was probably as good a place as any to start my analysis. The whole notion of life working like a formula is a child's-eye view of the world. X does not yield Y; life is much messier than that. Life simply is – without guarantees for any of us. What made me think God owed me?

Years earlier, a man working in the produce department at my grocery store asked me how I was. "OK," I told him dejectedly.

"You expected better?"

"Yes, actually I did."

The man pulled out a black marker and started drawing diagrams representing his faith on a produce box. He reminded me that everyone has obstacles to overcome, that life is challenging. At every juncture, there is a choice to be made between right and wrong, good and evil, light and dark. The right choice is not easy and does not come with rewards.

"Look at Christ's fate at the hands of a world that could not understand Him." The prophet in the produce section challenged me, "What makes you think you deserve better?" Somehow I had managed to forget that lesson.

Everyone is buffeted by strong winds from time to time. The tide goes out and then comes in again. The breath goes out and then comes in again. All of life is an ever-changing ebb and flow; it's the nature of the beast. And who am I to think I am entitled to something better than that? What makes me think anything could be better than that?

I began to look at things through a gentler lens. The Kuwaitis are fine. The Americans are fine. Even I am fine. I've been judgmental; I am human, I do the best I can. My ideas of right and wrong are provincial. As Jelaluddin Rumi, the famous Sufi poet, reminds me, "Out beyond ideas of wrongdoing and rightdoing, there is a field, I will meet you there." I was learning to relax into that field.

Chapter 18

Ya Darr, The Corrector, The Distressor

The Primary School Courtyard

At school the dysfunctional plot sickened. The principal, Barb, was supposed to meet with me every morning to help figure out coverage for missing staff members; she never showed. A staff meeting was canceled because she was at the senior management team meeting with the superintendent, except that meeting ended well before our staff meeting began. This particular meeting needed to happen. Our back-to-school night was the next day, and no planning had been done. We needed to collaborate with the Arabic Department which plays a very large role teaching our students Arabic language and religious studies, and participates in the back-to-school presentations. At the last minute, Barb changed the format for the evening without letting anyone know.

This apparently pushed the principal of the Arabic Department too far; he was very professional and easy to work with, so it took some doing to force him over the edge. He complained to the superintendent, with whom he was close. Khaled called me into his office (peremptory summonses had become de rigueur). "I want you to become the acting principal and report directly to me. Now," he announced. "Not next year, now." I was stunned.

Next he summoned Barb in to tell her, and required me to be present. This turned out to be one of the most difficult meetings I have ever had to endure. And I have attended more than my share of heart-breaking meetings; meetings informing parents of their child's suicide attempt, the possibility that their child is autistic, the news that their child has been sexually abused.

Khaled's reasoning for having me there was that my presence would force Barb to tell the truth. If she was not honest, I was used to confront her. His opening salvo with Barb this time was an inquiry into a teacher complaint made three weeks earlier when a computer disappeared from her classroom. Barb had not responded at the time; actually she said to me, "She should have locked her door, and it's just too bad she doesn't have a computer." The teacher was not well-liked; not by the administration, staff, parents, and definitely not by the students. Theft was rife in the school; every day someone came in my office and took the pad of post-its off my desk. Every day.

Yet in the meeting with Mr. Khaled, Barb was adamant in saying she had submitted the stolen property report, asking for a replacement computer for the teacher. Finally, at his insistence, she headed to her office, to fetch a copy of said report; only problem was that it came back dated the day we were speaking.

Mr. Khaled continued to grill Barb about what she had been doing the last few weeks, moving back and forth between conversational tones and shouting. She defended herself mightily. I did *not* want to be there, feeling that my presence added to her humiliation. I was now in the role of that unidentified man who witnessed my humiliation a few weeks earlier. Mr. Khaled and Barb went on and on, point/counterpoint; Khaled called in other people to challenge her claims. It was brutal.

Finally, after about two hours, he told her that he was transferring all authority to me. (He could have led with that ... this was not a discussion in which she could make her case.) He was not firing her, she would remain the principal, and I, the vice principal, for the rest of the year. She would keep her salary and benefits, kind of like the Queen of England, with the stipulation that she had to do whatever I told her or she would receive warning letters. Three warning letters and we're fired. In what I think was a sincere desire on Khaled's part to preserve Barb's dignity, the staff was not to be told of this change.

Barb was devastated and livid. Apparently, similar conversations between the two had occurred frequently last year as well. I tried to reassure her I had no idea this was coming and that I was truly sorry. I did know it might come the following year, but the first week of school, no. She retreated into immediate denial mode, and acted like nothing happened. She disappeared until the end of the day, when we had a staff meeting scheduled. She showed up for that, but did not participate. I probably would have gone home if I were in her shoes. Afterwards she made a point of outlining all the mistakes I made in the announcements.

I wondered if she would show up the next day. Although, if she was like most of us, she had no other job to go to.

I let Khaled know that I would need help to take on this new role and he promised to meet with me daily for a couple of weeks. I was pleasantly surprised when he followed through on this. I received a handbook that outlined a lot of the procedures for which I hadn't been able to get explanations. That alone increased my understanding of the organization exponentially. I also told him I wanted to move out of the "dorm," and not live with the staff members I had to supervise. I wanted help getting my driver's license, so I didn't have to wait a year before having independent means of transportation. (My daughter had doubts about my driving, but it had to be safer than relying on the bus and taxi drivers.)

Someone from the office would help me find a place; apartments cost more than my housing allowance, but not the two-thirds of my salary I was paying in the U.S. when I left. Plus it would be so worth it. I didn't like dorm life at 18, and it sure hadn't improved 40 years later. The new neighborhood would be closer to school, and have power that didn't come from the back of a truck. So that was all very good news, even though it might take a few months to get everything in place.

A week went by with me in my new job, and then payday arrived! I was really looking forward to my first paycheck, but oops, no pay. Everyone else got paid, but I didn't. Sometimes I feel like there's a little black rain cloud over my head. This inconsistency, however, was par for the course. I tried to appreciate the irony of being asked to take on the principal's duties at no extra pay while the principal earned $7000 a month for doing nothing. I'd have to wait until Sunday to try to sort it out.

The next week was another tough one. I stayed late on Sunday for Back-to-School Night, getting home way past my bedtime. Loss of sleep handicapped me for the rest of the week. We continued to be short staffed without substitutes. It ended up affecting every single classroom and every single member of the department. The tradition at the school was to complain, loudly and angrily, about everything. While the staffing challenges were definitely worth complaining about, it didn't stop there. There were complaints about the duty schedule, no playground for special needs, no swimming, fewer field trips, and on and on and on. Really, all of these complaints had merit, but none of them were in my control.

In the face of so many complaints, the ones about attending staff meetings were legion.

"Staff meetings end at 3:00, not 3:30." Which would have given us fifteen minutes for tackling the myriad problems facing the department.

"Well, according to your superintendent, the meeting goes until 3:30. Are you really telling me the superintendent doesn't know when the meetings end?" I had this misconception that if I were in a position of authority, people would listen to me. That turns out to be patently naive.

Finally, I called a short staff meeting that turned out to be quite brusque. No, let me be honest, I lost it. My frustration with the constant complaining about the same issues and the constant challenges about school policy erupted.

115

I suggested to the staff that they had a decision to make: would they trust me or not? I laid out the priorities as I saw them, first one being full staffing; we were still missing several teachers and teaching assistants. I told them I would fight for them, but that they needed to stop fighting with me. "You all are going to wear me out." Now I was complaining! Some people told me I was just experiencing culture shock, which was certainly part of the story. But the other part of the story was that some of the staff had transferred to special needs to find an easier gig. One teacher actually described himself as being semi-retired. Those teachers were strongly invested in ensuring that it would remain an easy gig.

It was a tense, adversarial meeting, and I am not proud of my behavior.

Immediately afterwards, I became gloriously and pitifully sick. (Can I use that as an excuse for my lousy conduct? No, I guess not.) There was a flu going around and I caught it. For a couple of days it had been masked by the large doses of ibuprofen prescribed to reduce the swelling in my ankle. By the time I got home, my temperature shot up four degrees. Then the ibuprofen sent my stomach into revolt. I ended up throwing up all over my one flat sheet in the middle of the night. It is lonely throwing up all alone, not that anyone really wants to witness it. I spent the next two days in bed.

By the third day, I began to feel a lot better, and decided to head to the market. I hadn't been to the big grocery store for two weeks as I was trying to let my ankle mend. The taxi driver didn't know how to get there, although Lulu's Hypermarket is a well-known landmark. It turned out he was brand-new to Kuwait, but between his friend on the phone and my gesturing, we finally got there.

I filled my shopping cart without incident, until I got to the produce section. Suddenly the sight of food revolted me. I asked where the nearest toilet was, knowing there wasn't much time. (My father always called bathrooms "toilets," which for some reason was profoundly embarrassing to me, but in Kuwait they are always toilets.) In that huge store, they were, of course, far, far away; way out past the check stands. I headed shakily in that direction, but didn't make it. My reusable green grocery bags were now un-usable vomit bags. The check-out people tried to put my groceries in them. "No, no you don't want to use those," I said, feebly.

A constant remark made to Westerners in the Middle East was, "No problem. Don't worry," even though the situation seemed extremely problematic for the Westerner. That day, I received a knowing nod of the head, "You have problem."

In the meantime, Shamiya School somehow carried on without me. "Get over yourself, Zanne." I received quite a few messages from staff filled with good wishes and notes that I was missed. That seemed miraculous, given the tenor of our last staff meeting. Either people were kissing up, or they genuinely missed me. It would be interesting to see what kind of fallout from the staff meeting I would have to deal with when I got back.

Chapter 19

Ya Bari', The Evolver

The Mess I Was In

The mosque back at the apartments was now hidden; only the two domes and the minaret peaked above the construction. The cricket players returned to the no-man's-land of the sand lot. Pedestrians picked their way through the piles of sand and trash. Buses, trucks and cars packed down roads whose surfaces morphed like a beach after a storm. The landscape was ravaged daily and life regrouped in the aftermath. After the daily storms at work, I felt pretty ravaged, too. The regrouping took enormous effort.

I developed a theory that if we treat people like children, they act like children. People felt controlled and disrespected at Shamiya School, and their response was to whine and complain. Even the principals and department heads, who met weekly with Mr. Khaled, acted like children vying for recognition from him. Being an optimist by nature, I hoped that as our special education staff became more empowered, and involved in real decision-making, they would feel less need to complain.

However, by mid-October the crazy factor at school had escalated beyond anything I could imagine. I realized I was not having fun at work. There were some beautiful moments and beautiful people, but the system was so dysfunctional that it truly boggled my mind. Variations on the theme I had attempted to leave behind in American public schools.

Staff, including myself, were consistently treated in ways that met the criterion for workplace bullying. In Kuwait, we were lied to, yelled at, intimidated, and humiliated. We were disciplined for incidents reported through vicious rumor which had no basis in reality. The abuse went top-down, bottom up and colleague against colleague, creating wildly unnecessary hardship and heartache. And I just wasn't seeing any indication that change was possible. To entertain this thought felt like blasphemy to me. I had always been the one who could find the best in any situation and forge a path through all difficulties. I believe that everyone can grow, learn and change, but my core beliefs were being challenged daily. I was staring at that rock of truth, again.

Having Khaled as a supervisor felt a lot like being in an abusive relationship. He was impulsive and made hasty decisions, which he expected the rest of the administrative team to support. He often changed his mind the next day, and couldn't understand why we were implementing the very tasks he had set for us the day before.

There were two Khaleds: Rational Khaled and Crazy, Angry Khaled. I liked Rational Khaled. He cared about our students, worked hard and wanted the school to be a good organization. Crazy, Angry Khaled was irrational, accusatory, and inconsistent. To be fair, I think the School Board, with its emphasis on profit and control, probably had a large hand in creating Crazy, Angry Khaled. I suspect the pressures on him were tremendous and that he had less control than the rest of us assumed.

I was being called into Mr. Khaled's office multiple times a day, and confronted with some gossip or complaint. I never knew, as I entered the door, if I'd be dealing with Rational Khaled or Crazy, Angry Khaled. I don't mind people being upset with me, it's part of the territory when you are an administrator. But if every remark made by the employee who "is just drinking coffee and handing out worksheets" forces an urgent confrontation, I am not on board. "Politics," said Khaled. "You have to take this gossip more seriously, and learn to be more political." It is possible that being political is, in fact, an essential job skill for an administrator. But it was not a skill I wanted to develop.

I felt schizophrenic; no matter what I did, I lost. Add to that working two jobs, Principal and Vice Principal, without compensation, and I was one totally unfulfilled Vice Principal. This was definitely not the calm, doable job I was seeking as a bridge to retirement.

Finally I decided to tell Khaled that I was not the right fit for this situation, and that I wanted to step down as acting principal. He responded with emotional blackmail, "You can't give up now. You'll be failing." It felt more like a choice to me than a failure, although a year earlier Khaled's tactic probably would have worked. I would have had to prove to him, and to myself, that I had not failed. I would have continued to tilt at windmills on a good day and bang my head against a brick wall on a bad one. But one thing I finally seemed to be learning was to treat myself with a little respect ... even if no one else would. The following few days were the only manageable ones I could remember in the last two and a half months.

The first order of new business was to inform Barb and Angella, the counselor, who was really the power behind Barb's throne, that I had stepped down. Together we forged a triumvirate and began planning how to move forward productively. First, we needed to repair the rifts that formed as staff members lined up to support either Barb or me. Because they had not been told about the change in command, no one knew why I suddenly ran all the staff meetings, and insinuated myself into all meetings with parents. It was surely seen as a gross power play on my part.

During our next staff meeting, Angella presented an allegory about people in high places pulling on puppet strings, playing one puppet against the other. But the puppets figured out what was going on, and started working together. We staged a coup. We knew we were taking a risk, but decided to go for it.

The next day Barb and I were summoned into Khaled's office where he had just spent at least half an hour raking Angella over the coals. I think this was the first time she had experienced Crazy, Angry Khaled and she was visibly shaken. Three staff members had gone directly to him after our meeting and told him exactly what was said. Khaled was furious and felt slandered by what he thought he heard. He wanted to know who was responsible. I told Khaled we had planned it together and were all responsible.

"I'm so sorry that you feel hurt; that was not our intention. But I think that appointing me principal without informing the staff inadvertently tore our department apart."

"We did that to protect Barb," Mr. Khaled reminded me.

"I know, and I understand that you were being respectful of Barb. But it was not seen that way by the staff. I didn't anticipate this either, but I continue to feel that the only way forward for our department is for me to step down."

Khaled eventually agreed and even owned up to his part in pitting Barb and me against each other. He also remarked that there was such a thing as too much honesty. I couldn't agree with him there. Part of the conflict for me was cultural; Kuwait is a very hierarchical place. I don't want to be a hierarchical leader; I know that what works is a collaborative, respectful environment of shared responsibility. The collaborative model is what I am interested in, I told Khaled, again acknowledging that I might not be the right fit for Shamiya School.

Following this kerfluffle, I gradually began to feel a bit free again. I had been assuming I was stuck in Kuwait for at least two years, although I only had a one year contract. Because I wanted to try another international placement, I had this idea I should stay longer. A short tenure doesn't look professional during interviews. Yet at that moment in time, with so much conflict at work, I didn't have the energy to do an international job search. Then it struck me that I could go back to the school where I worked in Washington State. I don't know why it hadn't occurred to me before.

This inability or reluctance to change plans is an ingrained pattern for me. It has something to do with honoring commitment.

When I left Washington, I had taken a leave of absence, so a job would be available to me if I chose to return. I didn't know what the job would be, but I would have one. And the Chimacum schools were looking a whole lot better from where I now sat. Later, if I wanted, I could apply to a real international school. My possibilities would be somewhat limited, as many countries, including China surprisingly enough, have age restrictions. But this option provided me with flexibility and time to figure out my next steps.

I suppose it's not so surprising that I had trouble shifting gears once I got to Kuwait. What I expected and what I encountered were wildly different. Everything had fallen into place so easily for me to go there that I had been convinced I was following the leadings of that still, small voice within. I was equally convinced that I was unassailable; that the integrity with which I lived would protect me. Not so much, as it turned out. To end up in such an abusive and unhealthy situation was a huge shock to me.

Kuwait was not the ideal work situation that would get me to retirement. But maybe it was my chance to choose taking care of myself over trying to make something work that was simply unworkable. Trying and trying to save unsalvageable situations was another pattern in my life. The thought of leaving made me a little sad, but also untied the enormous knot in my stomach. I hadn't had a knot in my stomach for years. I was proud of some of the work I was doing; I thought I had the skills to turn our department around. But I wasn't willing to put up with the bullying. I was finally past seeing this as an interesting challenge when it was really just a crazy-making situation. I'd had more than my share of those already. Perhaps I was shattering my ideals upon the rock of truth.

How to proceed from here? I made a conscious decision that I would not react defensively to the continued attempts to humiliate and intimidate. I would not counterattack, and I would not stop being friendly, even to those who did their best to breach my integrity. I would continue to expect accountability from the staff and from myself. I had nothing to prove to anyone, and I was doing a good job. A subset of the staff knew exactly what to do to keep improvements from happening, and they acted upon that knowledge with great efficiency. It was my own need to continue to bring as much good practice and kind relationship as I could to the school. In that way, I was unassailable and my integrity was intact.

Even with a plan to move forward at Shamiya School, I decided I would not spend more than a year in Kuwait. I missed my daughters, and the comfort of Port Townsend. I hadn't experienced the travel I had been looking forward to when I came to Kuwait because of paperwork issues. I still wanted to explore the world. Where would my next base of operations be, abroad or at home? I didn't know.

Chapter 20

Ya Muqit, **The Sustainer**

Leaving for Failaka Island

Another month rolled by, and the golden mosque disappeared completely. Every time I went out walking in the neighborhood, I had to take a different route around the new holes and ten foot high dirt piles. As the piles migrated, cars made new paths through the sand, and the cricket players shifted their playing fields. The external conditions of life mirrored the confusing, shifting landscape of my internal life as I continued to struggle with the randomness of work.

One weekend morning, I looked out the apartment window and saw a fight on the cricket field. Friends were pulling friends off each other, arms gesturing wildly, voices raised. Play almost resumed, but then the shouting started again. This is a country that loves to argue.

The principal at our high school, a regal Arabic

woman, told us about one of the fights that happened in her building. "The kid insulted his family; he had to fight him back," she said. Protecting family honor is a strong value in any country, but nowhere stronger than in the Middle East. And revenging a breach of honor is expected. It does make it difficult to promote conflict resolution, or even a physically safe environment at school.

A significant leak of hydrogen sulfide escaped from an oil well near the Iraqi border. It drifted toward Kuwait City, and although the government said it was safely within health limits, we had our doubts. I walked over to the neighborhood McDonald's. I needed their free wi-fi to load books on my electronic reader. Although it was only five minutes away, my eyes stung, my lungs hurt and I felt strange for hours afterwards. Clearly, staying inside for a while was the better part of valor. When I got back to school, I discovered one of our staff members was in hospital.

"What happened, April, are you ok?" I asked when she returned a week later.

"The doctors said I had sulfide poisoning." Sulfide poisoning is nothing to trifle with; it can cause bronchial constriction, loss of smell, and kidney damage. OSHA says that at 100 parts per million, death may occur within 48 hours. After I returned to the U.S., I found a news report on the leak. The oil company set the well on fire to reduce the spread of the sulfide. I never could find out how many parts per million we inhaled. The Emir assured us we were all safe.

On my own physical front, my ankle was finally getting better; it had been five or six weeks since I rolled it. All I had to do now was avoid twisting it again on an unexpected paving stone or piece of garbage. That was surprisingly difficult. The amount of garbage around Kuwait was staggering. There were a few neighborhoods that were a bit cleaner, but not because people took care of their surroundings. The residents in these areas continued to throw garbage everywhere, but hired expats to clean up after them. I felt mystified that a country that had been so heavily damaged in the war was completely uninterested in taking care of what they had now.

The weather must have gotten slightly cooler because I didn't have the AC on quite as much. I sat outside one evening with my friend, Mary, and had a meal in the dust of our neighborhood. There was a slight breeze and it was pleasant, though I was still soaked in sweat when I got home. Soon it would be cool enough to go to the beach.

Mary was a diminutive fireball from the U.K. She was a couple of years older than me, and had been in Kuwait for five years. She charged her way through the school wearing tulip skirts and demanding that teachers develop high quality lesson plans for the more mildly disabled students. The ones I thought I would be working with. We shared many points of view educationally and were at similar life stages. It made for a mutual admiration society, supporting each other in the face of a school that cared more about snazzy bulletin boards than substantive teaching. Her company was a real blessing.

"Maybe I'll go to the U.K. with her over the winter break," I thought. I wasn't comfortable traveling alone, and she was the only one I'd met who would be compatible. Most everybody at the school was about fifteen years old, or so they appeared to me.

I found making travel plans for the break intimidating, although I desperately needed a change of scenery. With no foreign travel experience came no experience planning an adventure abroad. And because I'd never been anywhere, every place sounded intriguing. Where to go? Our secretary invited me to visit her family's chalet in Egypt. People told me the best place to go for ancient sightseeing is Lebanon. *You will never have an opportunity like this again,* I told myself. *Push past this uncertainty and do something.*

By then, I had decided to try again for an overseas job in a better functioning school. Things had calmed down enough at work that I thought I could handle the job search. I renewed my membership in the organization that holds the job fairs and began researching schools and countries. Sending out resumes by the dozens occupied much of my downtime.

Back at school, the triumvirate was operating smoothly. Working with Barb and Angella was providing a lot of support for all of us. The constant call to the carpet in Mr. Khaled's office would come and we would look at each other and shrug. Afterwards, we could laugh together about the craziness. Barb still needed a lot of reminders to do her part. "Did you check your email?" Angella would ask. "You have to check it every day." While that seemed like an obvious thing that any administrator would do automatically, I was still happier to be working with her than undermining her, even if unwittingly.

My fondness for the staff continued to grow. One of them called me, "Zanne, *habibi,* (sweetie) I need you up here right now." This emergency call usually signaled extreme student behavior. Hitting, spitting, running away occurred with regularity. One student

128

liked to stick his finger up his butt and then wipe it on whoever was handy. So I grabbed my trusty yellow pad to document events, and headed upstairs. When I got there, I found a fabulous feast the Arabic teachers had prepared for all of us. Tears filled my eyes. They were the most generous people, taking time to share even in the midst of their incredibly hard workday.

These gifts notwithstanding, I couldn't see staying in such a crazy-making situation. The latest hierarchical edict decreed that all, repeat all, information must go through Mr. Khaled who would dole it out to the underlings whose job it was to deal with whatever needed to happen. No more talking directly to the person you needed to work with, that was just crazy talk. I took perverse pleasure in advising Khaled that our brand-new toilet would not flush away bowel movements; it would flush urine, but not bowel movements. I don't know if he got the irony, but I did amuse myself.

Throughout my life, I had always been the patron saint of Lost Causes, staying in situations long past hope of repair. I finally came to the realization that staying in abusive situations is not actually noble, but masochistic. Strangely, this was a difficult realization for me because I had the *Different Clan's* need to save the day, and the heartfelt belief that good communication could resolve any conflict. One more ideal shattering upon the rock of truth.

At about this same time, I was realizing that I probably am not cut out for being an administrator. In spite of Khaled's continued coaching, I can't/don't want to curb my honesty in favor of being more political. He had offered me the principal position, with full acknowledgment and benefits, for the following year.

Tempting as this might have been to me at one time, I knew I was not interested.

But what would I do? Knowing I had options gave me great psychological relief. I could go back to Chimacum the next year or take another year-long leave of absence. That would allow me to try a different international school, and still have a job to go back to if nothing worked out. This was a pressing issue because I was required to let Shamiya School know my plans by mid-December. It was just around the corner.

All the new staff got their residency status, and thereby their ability to leave the country, just as the next major holiday rolled around. Except me. I was absent on the day the medicals were done, so I still had little legal standing in Kuwait. The school held my passport, and I was mighty jealous of all those jetting off to Abu Dhabi.

The 10 day holiday, Eid Al Adha, honors sacrifice as exemplified by Abraham's willingness to sacrifice his son to God. As a parent, I find this most problematic. (I don't mean to be flippant, but this story has always been one I could not relate to. What parent is willing to murder their own child?) Like Christmas in the U.S., there was not much sign of sacrifice in Kuwait. Mostly people shop, travel and vacation, although several colleagues were headed to Mecca for Hajj. Every able-bodied Muslim is expected to make the pilgrimage at least once in their lifetime. "You must be so excited!" I enthused.

To my surprise they responded, "I know I need to go, but I'm not really looking forward to the trip." Hajj is not the quiet, contemplative experience I imagined. A noisy crowd of three million people retrace the steps of the Prophet Muhammad (Peace Be Upon Him), Abraham and Ismael. Wikipedia reports, "At densities above 6 or 7 persons per square meter, individuals cannot move, groups are swept along in waves, individuals jostle to find breath and to avoid falling and being trampled." It is, indeed, a commitment.

I spent some of Eid Al Adha planning a trip to Melbourne, Australia. Finally, I knew what to do. I would go to Melbourne where I could attend a job fair and look for a position in a different international school. Even though I was half-way around the world, Australia was still incredibly far away. It would be an expensive trip. I swallowed hard at the cost, and then excitement exploded. I had always wanted to go to Australia; Lily traveled there with a peace building organization when she was in middle school, and Addie and I were jealous. Now was my chance. I arranged to stay at the Quaker House to save money.

I hopped onto my computer, looking up things to do. (How did people plan travel before the personal computer? I can even check the weather before I go, and decrease my obsessing over what to pack by about half.) Much to my surprise, I discovered there are penguins in Australia; little, tiny ones that come to shore each evening after feeding in the waters around the southern coast. I have a soft spot in my heart for penguins. My friend, Emmi and I built a huge clay penguin when we were in third grade, praying it would not explode in the kiln. When it came out in one piece, we brought ginger ale "champagne" to school to celebrate. That penguin migrated from my house to her house every month for a very long time. Finally, it broke at Emmi's, but I forgave her.

The current, travel-less holiday gave me time to do more extensive exploring in Kuwait. One day, I went to the aquarium and saw the most amazing ray I'd ever seen. It was about three feet across and had a tail four feet long. But most impressive were its leopard skin markings. The tropical fish with their exploding colors were actually cuddling up in the soft coral and laying down. Really. I didn't know fish did that. Is it only aquarium fish, or do all of them (except sharks) take a break from time to time? It was pretty darn cute.

I confess that it was challenging to find anything to do in Kuwait that didn't involve shopping. I had lost enough weight that I needed new clothes (you know you've lost weight when your watch is too loose on your wrist). Mary took me to the most enormous mall I had ever seen. And it was the baby mall in Kuwait. No bargains to speak of as the Kuwaitis are so very wealthy. Nothing very funky either, so I didn't find much I liked.

Running errands always revealed more of the fascinating contrasts seen everywhere in Kuwait. Walking along the corniche (the promenade beside the water) by the science museum, I passed a covered woman towing her daughter who was in western dress complete with heelies (shoes with roller skate wheels in the heels). Mary and I saw a man at a restaurant who clearly had two wives; four are allowed by law. Everyone was dressed traditionally except one daughter whose skirt was so short … I don't want to say how short it was.

We lived south of Kuwait City, which put us closer to the undeveloped desert. And while the men wear white, which makes sense in a desert climate, the women invariably wear black. Black! What could be worse in all that heat? "Does Islamic law require that you wear black?" I asked one of the staff.

"No, but it is traditional; black is considered the most modest color, and it is important to be modest." Of course, many of the black *abayas* were beaded like evening gowns, so I doubt that fits the modesty guidelines. I didn't mention that.

Mary and I decided to go to Failaka Island just off the coast in the Persian Gulf, which has some ruins and traditional houses on it. The Greeks settled it at one point and named it Icarus, presumably for all the sun. We took a catamaran to get to it. I was looking forward to getting out of the city. The boat ride was pleasant and we pulled up to the little island at a rusty old dock. Like much of Kuwait, the place is in a terrible state of disrepair. There was garbage everywhere, and the former beach cottages were riddled with bullet holes; reminders of the first Gulf War.

We rode past camels, looking for the island's family beach. The family designation meant that Mary and I could go there and maybe even wear shorts. Tired old palm covered huts marked the beach, an ugly trash-strewn patch of sand. We didn't stay. The tiny museum, however, was quite nice and just about the only place in the country with a traditional Kuwaiti home. The architecture was similar to the American Southwest, with adobe style buildings. The main room was furnished with *diwaniya* cushions lining each wall, the floor covered with beautiful old carpets.

As we were looking around the compound, we came across a bridal suite. Three very old Kuwaiti women came in and started talking with us. "Where you from?" being the first question, of course. It turned out they were members of the royal family, and they identified themselves in the old photographs hanging on the walls. One of the women, the oldest and least cogent, absent-mindedly picked up a stick from the display, cleaned her teeth with it, and then replaced it. Nothing was behind glass, allowing for unlimited access. This was fun for visitors, but probably not so great for historical preservation. Meeting these wonderful women provided us with a glimpse into the merging of Kuwait's present and past and all the accompanying contradictions.

And then there was an exciting event: the weather broke. We had two days of real clouds, not smog. Next, lightning lit up the sky and two drops of rain fell. For two days following this momentous occasion, I could go out walking and not come home one big blob of sweat! It was heavenly. I couldn't believe it was November. Changes were on the horizon.

Chapter 21
Ya Muntaqim, The Avenger

A Gift From One of Our Students

Thanks to the Emir, we got an unexpected day off in November. One night, long after I had gone to bed and turned off my phone, Kuwait shot off 77,282 fireworks. The government staged the largest fireworks display ever recorded up until that time. It commemorated the 50th anniversary of the establishment of the Kuwaiti constitution, and cost 15 million dollars. Ironically, the Emir had just dissolved the parliament. As he looked out at the crowd, the story goes, he saw a young girl. Thinking how late she was staying up to watch the pyrotechnics, and how tired she would be in the morning, he decided to cancel school the next day.

A day off from school was a welcome gift. Kuwait didn't have a parliament, but we got a day off. Although the country is considered quite democratic by Gulf state standards, a commentary in Al Jazeera suggests it has "elections without democracy."

Curiouser and curiouser. I couldn't say much about that while in Kuwait; it would have created an international incident and resulted in losing my job.

I was trying to stave off a cold, so despite my sarcasm, I appreciated the Emir's gesture. It was great to go back to sleep. First, however, I got out of bed at five AM and got ready to go to work, still not turning on my cell phone. I trotted down to the bus, where a young teacher told me school was cancelled. After getting the news, he celebrated by drinking all night – in a country where drinking is illegal.

Clearly it was time to get over my distaste for being tethered to my mobile. I was near the top of the school phone tree now that I was a fancy administrator. I should have initiated 30 phone calls. Fortunately, even with my oversight, no one showed up for work.

The next week was a tough one; it seemed that the more I attempted to do the right thing, the angrier people became. The speech and physio-therapists had asked for an additional position for their staff. In order to make this recommendation to the superintendent, we needed to document the need. So the triumvirate, Barb, Angella and I, calculated the number of hours the therapists spent with students. It turned out that number was significantly lower than anyone else on staff; one of the them saw kids for only about half the time students were in school. "We work harder than anyone else in the department, in the whole school!" one asserted angrily. They worked one-on-one with students, unlike everyone else, and even then refused to work with those with behavioral problems. "Fix the kids' behavior, then we can work on language therapy." One reason students act out is because they have no way to communicate their needs. Whose needs come first anyway? The therapists and I disagreed on the answer to that question.

"This is the group I told you was sitting around drinking coffee and handing out worksheets," Khaled told me. And indeed, I often stumbled on people with their feet up on their desks and their eyes closed. No students in sight. When you stir a hornet's nest, you tend to get stung. The staff, not unexpectedly at this point, went to Khaled to complain. I was duly lectured on being more political even though he agreed there was no need to hire additional therapists.

The department secretary, who I loved, was also angry with me. I knew what a mistake it was to run afoul of the one person who keeps an office functioning. Unfortunately, she had been missing in action, a lot; she was never in the office. Because Fayrah kept everything locked up and became irate if you rummaged for supplies, this was a major problem. What were we to do when a parent needed to sign a student out early and the early dismissal slips were securely locked away? Or help a parent who didn't speak English. An Arab speaker needed to be in the school office at all times. I gently reminded her, "Please let me know if you are going to be out of the office. Barb and I have staff evaluations to do and will be not be around much." Again, what was I thinking? Fayrah was furious and refused to speak to me or do any work that related to my set of tasks. So much pettiness. So much work avoidance. Fayrah had been strongly in my corner as long as I did everything she wanted me to do. When I needed to be a supervisor with her, her behavior morphed into furious obstructionism.

That week I participated in my first Kuwaiti PTA meeting. A small, but dedicated group of parents sat with me in the auditorium, which, to my surprise, continued to stink of cat urine. (Why we didn't close the auditorium doors when it was unoccupied remained unclear.) The parents wanted to see the school improve; they felt the administration did not listen to them or consider the needs of their children, a common theme in most schools. I was able to outline our plans to upgrade curriculum and teaching practices within the Special Needs Department. I also let parents know that other departments were struggling due to lack of materials and good teaching practices. We had a very open and honest exchange. It was truly a delight, though possibly dangerous. I didn't know if my remarks would get back to Khaled, provoking another dressing-down in his office. It felt so good to talk with people who shared the goal of children's growth that the risk seemed worth it.

For stress management, I went for a Thai massage; Mary introduced me to this place and the women there liked me. If Mary went alone, they always asked where I was. Maybe it wasn't affection, maybe they just recognized the sad condition of my musculature. My muscles had been in a perpetual state of tension for decades, and the extreme stress of my current job didn't help. Neither did the hard bed, the lack of suspension in the buses that took us back and forth to school and the general lack of any comfort in our apartments. The tiny, strong Thai women did their best for me.

We were approaching a three-day weekend celebrating the New Year. It was Thanksgiving time back home, but that holiday has no equivalent in Kuwait. It felt strange to hear about my friends' and family's Thanksgiving plans. The temperature was still in the mid-90s most days, though I did put my blue jeans on for the first time. It was too hot for denim, but I just had to do it. There was a rare appearance of clouds during part of the day. Clouds were as uncommon as the sun in the Pacific Northwest in November.

Over the weekend, I shared a meal with a couple of friends and watched a *dhow* (a traditional wooden boat) pull out of the harbor. The lines remained elegant though it was now powered by engines. Pearl diving and trade were the activities that originally established this region. Fishing was important as well – another similarity to the Northwest.

I sent off a batch of letters of interest to schools and was looking forward to the job fair in Australia. Not to mention seeing the penguins. Staying with the Quakers in Melbourne provided a good opportunity to sit with Friends again. I hoped it was an un-programmed (silent) meeting as I craved quiet after living in this loud and raucous society.

December arrived, and I went out into the beautiful, sunny day in my shirtsleeves. I wandered around my neighborhood and took photos for people back home. I was ready to share the gritty details: the grim apartment buildings, the piles of garbage, the empty lots that resembled landfills. Old furniture, plastic bags and God knows what were strewn everywhere. There was no vegetation, no sidewalks; just a wasteland with apartment buildings plopped down in the middle. I had held off on taking photos as I didn't want to worry my friends and relations. But enough time had passed that I figured people, notably my children, knew I was safe and surviving, and wouldn't be too freaked out when they saw actual images.

Hiba, a Syrian friend from work, invited me to

go out into the desert with her family. We were to barbecue and hang out around the fire. Just my style, and I was excited to be getting out of the city.

The "desert" turned out to be another sandy, unbuilt section in the middle of town right next to a major highway. Like where I lived. It was basically a big parking lot filled with cars and families, all grilling and playing ball and riding bikes. Not quite what I expected. The extended family is the context in which almost all socializing occurs. "When a woman marries a man," Hiba told me, "she is really marrying his family. She spends most of her time with his female relatives, whether she wants to or not." Socializing generally occurs in same gender groups, and it is unusual for women and men to gather together unless they are family. It's not unheard of, however, for young people to sneak text messages to someone of the opposite sex when they are out.

It was great fun to be with Hiba, who is an irrepressibly strong, enthusiastic young woman. I met her entire family. Only a couple of them spoke English so my ability to communicate was limited. We ate premade hamburgers, chips and hummus.

The style of dress varied tremendously within her family. Some of the men and women dressed traditionally and others, including Hiba, wore western attire. Hiba said she liked to show off her cute figure. She was quite the rebel. Apparently the husband generally decides how his wife will dress, although I suspect Hiba's husband may have been less in control of this area than some.

Hiba's younger sister, who was eighteen, had just started college. Yesterday a woman came to the family home to examine her as a marriage prospect; the son did not come this first time.

"I'm so excited," she bubbled. "His mother said I was very beautiful." Which she was. I had trouble imagining myself in her situation even though marrying for love had not worked out so well for me.

Hiba's husband cheated on her so she tried to divorce him. A couple has to divorce three times in Kuwait before it's final. The husband claimed the first time was under duress. Which, in fact, it was, because Hiba's father threatened to kill him. And then her brother flew in from Australia to emphasize the point. She stayed for the children.

Hiba had not been back to Syria in a long time. Her uncle was killed by sniper fire while I was there, and she was working tirelessly to bring another relative over the border. This happened long before Syria became news in the States. It's one thing to read about sniper fire in the news, and quite another to hear it from someone real that I cared about. One of our secretaries at work had a Syrian fiance who was a soldier in the Assad regime. He was kidnapped by resistance fighters who demanded a ransom from relatives in Kuwait. The relatives did not have the money. His ear was mailed to them when they failed to pay; then he was murdered. These families are just like you and me; or maybe they have even less political motivation, and certainly less money, than many Americans. All they wanted to do was love and care for their families.

Sitting in the desert with Hiba's family, I realized I don't have nearly the social stamina that would be required in an Arabic family. I found it tiring to be the focus of such intense interest for a long time, especially when the language barrier was so great. I made my apologies and Hiba drove me back to my drab apartment in the dust.

Work continued to be interesting in the oddest ways. The deadline for informing the school about plans for the upcoming year had passed, so people now knew I had decided not to return. Khaled called me into his office on two different occasions to ask why. "I heard you said you were leaving because of how I treated you," he accused probingly. Someone was still trying to rat me out.

"I'm interested in a more collaborative model," I explained truthfully. "The model here at Shamiya is not a good fit for me."

He grudgingly responded, "I didn't think it was your style to blame me, and I really do think you're doing a good job."

In the next breath, however, emotional blackmail reared its ugly head; "I can see that you stopped working as soon as you stepped down as Principal," he barked. I disagreed and told him that many staff members were coming to me, suggesting that I was working too hard. Hard work was not necessarily seen as a virtue. He said teachers were unhappy; I told him at least four staff members came to me in the last week, saying how pleased they were to be working with me. And in fact, nearly every single staff member approached me at one time or another asking me to stay on. Khaled's swift hundred and eighty degree shifts of viewpoint were constant. It was hard to keep up with whatever current attribution he might assign to me.

The current school disaster was that Khaled decided we couldn't send kids home when they engaged in violent behavior, such as fighting, hitting, spitting, headlocks and choking. These behaviors happened almost daily, and some of the students were bigger and stronger than any of us on staff. I have always held that we need to keep our word that school is a safe place. No child should have to worry about being hurt at school. From a teacher's point of view, I know as well as anybody how awful it is to be alone facing that kind of behavior. Being in that position frequently in U.S. public schools was one of the reasons I had been looking for a new gig in the first place.

If we can't send them home, and we can't restrain them, which is dangerous for students and staff, what do we do in the face of violent behavior? Kids discover very quickly that teachers have no serious interventions. Even the severely intellectually disabled, non-verbal students waited until only one teacher was in the room before acting out. It was incredibly frustrating. But I kept trying to do the best I could. I was committed to supporting teachers and kids, plus I would be bored if I just sat around.

In December, the school sponsored a big conference day for educators throughout Kuwait. Recognizing that use of external motivators was the gold standard in Kuwait, I decided to design a workshop on *internal* motivators for the occasion. All the punitive things that the administration and board did at Shamiya School were internal motivation killers, according to a now-large body of research. For example, requiring people to sign in and out of school discourages people from working late. Offering monetary rewards for perfect attendance, discouragement of creativity, innovation and taking initiative are examples of policies that drastically reduce internal motivation. This workshop was my little piece of subversion. I seemed to require at least one good act of rebellion a month, even though it went unnoticed. I ended up on Kuwaiti television, twice, though I never saw it. Ironically, Mr. Khaled told me I had a gift for training.

Chapter 22
Ya Qahar, The Ever Dominant

Trees in Australia

Later in December, work went from toxic to hellish. I had been working closely with Barb and Angella, and our relationships were cordial when we commiserated. However, I quickly tired of complaining; I wanted to do something useful. We were encountering one consistent problem in specialist classes. For art, music and PE, two academic classrooms were combined to provide common planning time for teachers. While this was a theoretically sound plan, there were invariably serious fights between students from the different classrooms.

A few weeks earlier the triumvirate had agreed on switching the schedule around to separate two classes and end the fighting. No one followed up on it. It involved secondary classes and the new division of labor had me in charge of elementary, so it was not my responsibility to follow through. But I am task-oriented to a fault, and when I came across the suggestion in my

145

notes, I brought it up at one of our daily meetings. Should I go ahead with it? Barb and Angella said yes. I touched base with all the teachers involved. They discovered a simple way to fix the problem through a minor schedule change. All teachers affected said they were willing to work with the changes. The art teacher would teach one class on Tuesdays, a day on which he had no classes. Why he had an entire day with no teaching responsibilities remained a mystery to me. But he said the change was fine with him.

All schedule changes had to go through Mr. Khaled, so my plan was to be sure it was doable and then ask for permission. Although I confess I did consider doing it on my own because he was so controlling, and this was such an easy fix. Before I could even commit that faux pas, I was hauled into his office. Barb was there. "Are you changing the schedule?" Mr. Khaled demanded. "You have no authorization, and Barb knows nothing about this. All schedule changes must go through me." He was livid. I was stupefied, hurt and angry that Barb would hang me out to dry over this.

I said, "Barb, we sat together yesterday afternoon, we discussed the possibility, and I asked you if I should go ahead and look into it. You said, 'Yes.'"

She replied, "I knew nothing about this. And besides I have lots of teachers coming to me saying they will leave the school because of how you treat them, and I can't afford to lose good teachers."

I could not believe it. I didn't want to believe it. But apparently Barb would say anything to make herself look good. I had thought the triumvirate was working well together. I remarked that I thought it was a good thing to try to solve a problem and prevent fighting, but that did not impress. By the end of the meeting, I was in tears and as angry as I've ever been. I couldn't do anything useful at Shamiya School without pissing somebody off.

I had been taken by surprise when some of the Arabic staff used attacks on colleagues to further their own status. Then I was dumbfounded when some of the western staff adopted this norm as well.

Angella was the next to attack me. She said, "Teachers are complaining about you."

"What are they complaining about?" I asked.

"They think you're condescending."

"What makes them say that?"

"Well, you have a tone."

"Can you give me an example? It's hard to work on a tone I don't know that I have."

"You have a tone in staff meeting," she threw at me.

"In staff meeting I raise my voice to be heard. I slow down and simplify my speech a bit so the Arabic staff, with their limited English, can understand."

"That offends the western staff."

"So I should ignore over half of our staff?" I asked incredulously.

Angella didn't reply to my question, but she was not done. "Well, there was the time you went into the twelfth grade classroom. That isn't really your responsibility, it's Barb's."

"You and Barb were out of the office. The

teacher called me directly to help deal with an out of control student."

"But the method you used was inappropriate for the age group."

"The method I used is appropriate for anyone. When people are in a high state of emotional arousal, they are not processing verbally. One way of de-escalating the situation is to draw what happened while you talk about it. Visual processing is almost always easier for people."

"Well, this was not a third grade student," Angella insisted.

"It worked immediately with the twelfth grader; even I was surprised."

"He would have calmed down anyway."

"Then why did the teacher call me?" The complaints went on and on like that. Dully, I realized our alliance no longer existed, and I had been dethroned.

At the same time, the Special Needs secretary, Fayrah, began to block work coming out of my office. I suspect this began because of a conversation we had a few mornings earlier. I was in a meeting with a parent when a long, protracted shouting match between Fayrah and one of our staff members erupted. I was embarrassed that a parent would be subjected to this loud display of dysfunction in our department. It is possible I was the only one disturbed, and that this kind of confrontation is culturally normal in Kuwait.

I talked to both Fayrah and the other staff member and let them know how seriously their shouting affected my conversation with the parent. The argument revolved around the teacher's access to a printer. He needed to turn in hard copies of lesson plans to meet a deadline. I had told everyone, including Fayrah, that staff members could use my printer any time. Fayrah disagreed.

This incident represented a major difference between our views regarding the role of administration. My philosophy was that we were there to support teachers and make their lives easier in any way possible. Her philosophy was that she needed to control resources and see that as few were used as possible. This resulted in the locking away of forms, printers and materials. Even opportunities for parents to make appointments were curtailed by her behavior. Remembering that we had problems with theft, I could almost understand this viewpoint. However, it required that she be in the office in order for staff to acquire the materials they needed. She was seldom to be found.

The Egyptian teacher involved was apologetic and cooperative. Next, I told Fayrah how embarrassed I had been in front of the parent. I gently asked her if she was all right; she had been expressing a number of health concerns. I noted that she was usually very skilled when talking with parents, and so I had been surprised. She responded mildly at the time, but from that moment on, she refused to speak to me, even to say hello. If I needed to set up a family meeting, which had to be done in Arabic, she refused. If I asked for the key to the cabinet so I could store materials, she said I was not her boss, and that the cabinet belonged to her. Actually, I was her boss and the cabinet didn't belong to her, but facts didn't matter. All three of my office mates were now actively interfering with my work and sabotaging my relationship with the superintendent.

The climate was toxic, hostile, obstructionist. If I had not tried to do my job, I might have been left alone. As it was, the mere act of showing up for work every day and accomplishing a task was grounds for abuse. I was outraged that people would act this way. I simply could not fathom it. Still I held onto my determination not to attack back, not to take it personally, even though the behavior was expressly designed as a personal attack. Most importantly, I would not take out my frustration on students or other staff. I continued to smile, say good morning for weeks in the face of derisive responses from my office mates. As Barb, Angella and Fayrah blocked any work I tried to accomplish, I was forced to pull back from administrative tasks. It was hard for me; I'm not good at looking busy. I went into classrooms as often as possible. I taught demonstration lessons, consulted about behavior and differentiation of instruction, and even helped do reading assessments in the elementary school. I tried to be a force for good.

However, I could not find a productive way forward for anything. And I was mad. I don't get angry very often, but I was angry! I had felt unassailable when I came to Kuwait. I believed that integrity protected me, and yet, I was attacked – for being cheerful, knowledgeable, for getting things accomplished. It dawned on me that I would be attacked if I were cranky, ignorant and never accomplished a thing. Perhaps naively, I continued to assume that people mean what they say. But that is not always the case. Some people don't want excellence if it prods them to change the way they do things. Some don't seek continuous improvement or look for more effective ways to do more with less. They may support surface measures like bulletin boards, but real innovation? No thanks! I had to accept that to many people, I didn't appear as a person with integrity; I appeared as a major pain in the ass. That was a bitter pill to swallow.

I began to recognize a pattern. Throughout my life, I had often felt misunderstood, and unjustly judged. In my apartment in Kuwait, I did some work with archetypes from a book by Caroline Myss, an intuitive healer. According to her framework, the archetype of Victim is strongly connected with how I relate to the world. That drew me up short as I do not like thinking of myself as a victim. I work hard to avoid that stereotype in spite of the abusive personal situations I have experienced. I don't even think of myself as a "survivor." I am much more than the fallout of the abuse. Yet there was that big Victim archetype right at the intersection of me and the outside world.

What did it mean that my relationship with the outer world was so heavily influenced by the Victim? Was my sense of being misunderstood a form of victimhood? Perhaps I needed to accept the world on its own terms instead of constantly trying to bend it to my own idealistic dreams. This would mean accepting people on their own terms. Not necessarily agreeing with them, but recognizing them for who they are rather than who I would like them to be. I wondered if I could accept others without judging them. Could I protect myself from them without judging them? How do I make a realistic assessment of a person and whether I can have a healthy relationship with them without feeling guilty? After all, the *Different Clan* is kind and accepting. I wanted to maintain those good values and make observations rather than judgments. Maybe that would enable me to stop reprising the victim role of the misunderstood, valiant champion. That would be nice. Maybe it was time to stop impersonating a superhero and join the human race.

With all this rolling around my brain, I got ready to go to Melbourne. As I was licking my wounds, my residency papers finally came in – a mere two weeks before flying out. I was so demoralized at this point that I decided if I could find another job, I would leave Kuwait in January. But if I broke my contract and went home, I'd never have a chance to get another international job. I continued to nurse the notion of finding a good international placement. I knew my experience at Shamiya School was not typical.

I was nervous about the trip to Australia. I had never traveled abroad before and here I was heading out alone. At least everyone would be speaking English. And I couldn't wait to get a change of scenery, see some trees and wildlife, walk some beaches. Perfect for me. I'd finish off the trip at a job fair and see if any good opportunities turned up. I'd try to discern some positive way forward.

Chapter 23
Ya Khafid, The One Who Humbles, The Softener

Quaker House, Melbourne, Australia

Another 20 hour flight; time to break out those support hose again. I wanted to be excited about the trip to Australia, but in truth, I was bruised and dazed from the constant onslaught at work. People say everything happens for a reason – I'm not entirely convinced. Some things seem random, just part and parcel of life. I am comforted by the Buddhist view of life as suffering. At the same time I know the beauty is right there by its side.

I can't really imagine God, or The Great Mystery, wanting us to be unhappy, sitting around cooking up problems for us. "Hmmm. I wonder what I could do to really screw up Zanne's life. Oh, I know. I'll have people yell at her and publicly malign her character." God laughs. I do believe God laughs a lot, but not at that kind of stuff. Then God would be like the host of America's Funniest Home Videos, and that kind of humor is just plain mean. There's a flavor of blaming the victim to the philosophy that everything happens for a reason. It implies that you need, even deserve, this suffering to occur. No one needs cancer, loss, or abuse in their lifetime, but we all get something.

If it's true that things happen randomly, I still have a role to play. It's my responsibility to wrestle as much learning and growth as I can out of whatever happens in my life. As Sartre said, "Freedom is what you do with what's been done to you." So what was I to be learning in this FOG (Fucking Opportunity for Growth) I was in?

I left the United States in search of a job I could sustain. I was too young to retire, and teachers, especially teachers who are single parents, don't have money. I had stewarded my small salary well, but there was only so much I could do. I needed a way to sustain myself that did not sap every living ounce of physical and spiritual energy out of me. Kuwait, as it turned out, was not it.

As I flew toward Australia, I mulled things over. I couldn't understand why people were so aggressive toward me. I brought a lot of experience to the table. I excelled at staff development. Evaluation data from previous jobs reassured me when the attacks plunged me into doubt. I had been careful at Shamiya to be supportive, and gather staff input as often as possible. There were people who clearly enjoyed working with me, and earnestly encouraged me to come back the following year. They appreciated innovation, good practices and high expectations. Then there were the ones who didn't.

I didn't want to believe the toxicity was the result of people being unable and unwilling to work together. Whether in the States or Kuwait, I was always stunned that people sacrificed the greater good of students for the sake of petty power struggles. That if they didn't get their way they would take their ball and go home. Or in Kuwait, they would take their ball, smash it in my face, and then tell the superintendent I stole it.

I had never experienced feeling as though someone simply hated me, and would do anything to make my life more difficult. Although not defending myself, not attacking back, and remaining friendly were important behavioral statements for me to make, there was no satisfaction for me in those responses. I held my ground on professional issues out of integrity and my belief in standing up to bullies. While in my mind, I had not done anything to merit this treatment, the whole situation put knots in my stomach that I had not had to untie for years. What was I to learn from this? Why was I constantly getting myself into situations where I had to battle so hard just to keep my footing? Where was the slip between the intentions in my cup and the bitter brew passing through my lips?

I was tired; deep down to the marrow of my bones tired. Schools in Australia and New Zealand start their academic year in January; maybe I would jump ship if I could find a job with a January start date. I hardly recognized this person who was willing to break a contract. I had always been overly responsible in meeting all my obligations; I would never leave an organization in a bind. After a while, it became too much to process, so I lost myself in a good book and, later, in sleep.

Toward the end of the flight, I got talking with a

woman sitting near me. The plane was arriving late, and I wasn't prepared to drive in the dark to get to Quaker House where I was staying. She offered to let me come to her house; "I have kids, it will be safe there." Sometimes I believe that I am too careful, so I wondered if I should take her up on her offer.

Be open to the possibilities that present themselves, I coached myself. It certainly would help me financially; I had not expected to take such an expensive trip, and now I had another night in a hotel. I finally decided I would accept the offer, but when we landed she disappeared. I made my way to the airport hotel and collapsed into bed, wondering if I had just had a narrow escape.

The next morning, I trooped back to the airport to rent a car, and begin the adventure of driving on the left hand side of the road. In a big city. In a big city I did not know. In a big city I did not know, all by myself. Interchanges and left hand turns were confusing, but I bumbled my way to Quaker House without too much difficulty. Driving on the left took a lot of concentration; I only went down the wrong side of the road twice. Only once was really scary.

Quaker House is a beautiful old home filled with leaded glass and topped with a clay tile roof. A flower garden bursting into bloom surrounded it, offering the perfect place to read outdoors. It was conveniently located near a lot of the places I wanted to go. I had a beautiful bedroom about the size of my entire apartment in Kuwait. The weather was sunny and in the high 60's; there were trees and flowers everywhere. The air and water were clean, and I could spend time outdoors. The sky was blue, and people were smiling. The dress was informal, and I pulled on my blue jeans again. There were thrift shops and funky clothes and bathing suits on the beach. I was in heaven! I had not realized how much the physical environment in Kuwait was affecting me.

It felt strange being there by myself at Christmastime. Throngs of people were out celebrating with friends and family. But I love to explore and there was plenty of that to do. My first explore was to the thrift shops. I poked around, listening to the wonderful Australian accents and finding skirts and jeans and even an interview outfit for the job fair later in the week.

My other priority was to see the little penguins that come ashore each night in Melbourne. (They have recently been renamed "little" rather than "fairy" penguins. It's about time.) I walked down to the St. Kilda breakwater in the daytime so I could scope out the observation site. There is a long city beach there with a cement boardwalk, cafes and skateboarders. I wandered down to the end of the breakwater reading all the signs about the penguins. A penguin docent showed me one little guy that had decided not to go out fishing that day. He was only about 13 inches high and a deep, deep blue/black and white. In a word, adorable. I made plans to come back at sunset when the rest of the penguins would converge on shore for the night.

The wind was whipping by the time I returned to the breakwater. I got there early enough to have a front row seat; I was followed by hordes of people. I don't do very well in crowds – I'm kind of short, and often feel overwhelmed. People of all ages gathered to penguin watch. I always love it when a wide range of generations come together. Night fell and the sky and water turned black. We all waited excitedly for the penguins to arrive. We saw a couple waddle onto shore and into the stones of the breakwater. I would rather have seen hordes of penguins than hordes of people, but that's how it goes with wildlife. They don't keep to a schedule. I was glad I had gotten a good look at the one during the daytime when I was the only human out. I went back to Quaker House tired and happy.

Chapter 24

Ya Jabbar, The Restorer, The Repairer

Abbotsford Convent, Melbourne

The next morning the librarian of the Quaker meeting arrived to put flowers around the house for the Sunday meeting for worship. A button I gave to a Quaker friend at home reads, "Never underestimate a feisty old Quaker." In Amelia, I was meeting another Friend with more strength than met the eye. She looked to be in her 80's, and had lost her husband a few years earlier. She shared what that had been like for her, how she manages to go on. She talked with me about the plight of the Aborigines in Australia, and how she and other Quakers had worked to support their rights. And she generously asked me how I was doing. Very few people in the world actually ask about the person they are meeting; Amelia was one of them.

If it's in my head, it usually comes out my mouth, so I told her about my struggles in Kuwait. Amelia was sympathetic, but, in good Quaker fashion, was sure I would discover strength in the midst of adversity, and lessons to lead me further down my spiritual path.

I hoped I found them soon so that when I returned to Kuwait I would know how to conduct myself. At that particular moment in time, I could not begin to see what a good next step might be. My adversaries were so committed to their opinions and complaints that nothing I did seemed to make any impact. Did that mean I just had to endure? Was that even a healthy stance for me, or was it capitulation to more abuse? I had not a clue.

I trundled off to bed and didn't wake up again for another 36 hours. I was disoriented; I'm a champion sleeper, but how could I possibly have slept so long? I wandered groggily into the Quaker library in the next room. Quakers believe in continuous revelation and are prolific writers. Every Quaker meeting has a library full of testimonies from the practical to the mystical, written by historical and contemporary Quakers. I idly picked up one by John Yungblut, a friend/Friend of several of my friends/Friends in Port Townsend, though I did not know that at the time. He was suffering from Parkinson's disease and cancer toward the end of his life and in "Hallowing Our Diminishments," he quoted Teilhard de Chardin:

> When the signs of aging begin to
> mark my body (and still more when
> they touch my mind), when the ill that
> is to diminish me or carry me off
> strikes from without or is born within

160

me; … at that last moment when
I feel I am losing hold of myself
 and am absolutely passive
within the hands of the great unknown
forces … O God, grant that I may
understand that it is You … *who is*
painfully parting the fibers of my being
in order to penetrate the very marrow
of my substance and bear me away
within Yourself … (Italics mine.)

I was not dying physically, but I was definitely battered and bruised, and feeling that nothing but the "great unknown forces" could help me now. And in the mere moment of reading this passage, I suddenly saw all that had happened in Kuwait as God "painfully parting the fibers of my being in order to penetrate the very marrow of my substance." I was cleft in half, allowing more forgiveness and love to penetrate, and then radiate from my being. To radiate into the hearts even of those who misjudged and attacked me. The anger left. What remained was the knowledge that love paved the way forward.

But there was more. John Yungblut was no slacker. He went on to write, "Jesus was able to love much because he had been forgiven much by God." Clearly I, too, have been forgiven much. God has patiently offered countless opportunities for me to let go of ego, and accept myself as a fallible human being. I, however, continued to try to be perfect and *Different*. Without perfection, I felt unworthy. Yungblut proposed that all my imperfections were already forgiven by the Great Mystery. Could I also forgive them? That would be the challenge.

He continued, "Forgiveness makes possible a deeper communion than that which existed before … It invariably releases love, and love is the energy of creation." I recognized that it was time to let go of quixotic quests and idealistic cravings and simply love, with the sole purpose of unleashing that energy of creation.

Forgiveness needs to be extended so much more often than most of us realize. I had practiced it when dealing with the people who hurt me in the past, releasing the choke hold trauma might have had on my life and my emotions. This allowed me to love and trust and live without fear. I had even forgiven myself (though that was the hardest work of all) for not being "smart enough" to avoid abuse, for introducing abuse into the house where my children lived.

It occurred to me that day in Australia that I had never forgiven God. I was incredulous as I realized I carried a sense of "This is my life? Seriously? I don't deserve this!" Beneath that was a resentment that I had dealt with *so* much, and a resignation to life always being a burden. My childish notion of the Golden Rule as equation left me with an expectation of receiving a reward for the difficult things I had endured, the hard work of recovery in which I had engaged. Where was my happiness, my joy, the beautiful relationship I wanted so much? I stamped my proverbial foot petulantly. I took such umbrage at not having my reward that I neglected gratitude, appreciation and reverence for my own life – not life in general, but my own.

And there are so many things to appreciate, revere and be grateful for: my children, the love of my friends, the peace of prayer and meditation, sublime moments mixed in with the painful ones. A rich life filled with small graces which it is surely my blessing to enjoy.

They say that lightning never strikes the same place twice. But I have been struck many times. Sufi teachers regularly remind their students to "die before death and resurrect now." Die to the ego, pride, and hubris, and enjoy the Kingdom of Heaven, Nirvana, Reality, here and now. I now framed the entire debacle in Kuwait as the Great Mystery "painfully parting the fibers of my being" in order to diminish my attachment to accomplishments, such as "expertise," and pride in work. Work was the one area of my life in which I had always excelled, which was untainted by the personal tragedies I had experienced. I had held on hard to this area of competence. If non-attachment is the secret to the cessation of suffering, here was one honking chunk of attachment that needed to go.

What made me think I was the one that could be the catalyst for change anyway? What super-power did I have that gave me the ability to change Shamiya School in Kuwait, or the public schools in the U.S.? Certainly these attitudes reeked of hubris. And, obviously, I learn the hard way – I had to be out and out attacked before I could let go of my arrogance, and really accept my status as a normal human being. At long last, I laid down my membership in the *Different Clan.*

Clearly, I was not going to change how things operated at Shamiya School, and the school was just as clearly not headed toward change on its own. If I had seen the slightest indication that improvement in the treatment of staff and students was possible, I would have stayed and contributed to the best of my ability.

My way forward was now clear. Right then and there, I forgave the people at Shamiya School who were attacking me. Even in the face of the impropriety, unfairness and irrational nature of their actions, and it wasn't hard to do. I wanted to be a source of love, and the only way to release more love was to forgive. The only thing any of us need to do in life is muster as much kindness and compassion for those in our path as we possibly can. That is what will save the world, in little, quiet, overlooked ways in a million little corners of the world.

I would go back to Kuwait, understanding that I was not in charge, I did not have to "do" anything; the Great Mystery would have its own way of teaching all those people whatever it was they needed to learn. I was not put on earth to fix them; I barely know how to fix myself. I barely know what I'm supposed to do or be at any given moment in time, let alone what someone else should do or be. What a relief to relinquish this burden of saving the world. I did not need to change the situation; I could not change the situation no matter how hard I tried. Any efforts in that direction would probably make things worse.

This, then, was the lesson Amelia was confident I would receive. I was grateful to discover a way to look at my experiences that led me toward a positive path at work, and a deeper understanding of myself and life. It was not a passive path, but a different one. I took a sharp turn off the Way of Control and veered onto Love Alley. The next day, I went to meeting for worship full of grace and gratitude. I sat in silence with Quakers I had never met before and felt at peace and full of light, so much light it spilled out all around me.

Chapter 25

Ya Hasib, The Accounter, The Reckoner

Twelve Apostles, Great Ocean Road, Australia

John Yungblut made it possible for me to release my tension, hurt and confusion. I could now frame my experience in a way that had meaning for me. No worries, mate. And just in time to explore an extraordinary continent. Australia is so vast and varied that it truly amazes. I knew I only had time to poke around the Melbourne area, and there was so much to see there that I suffered no hardship.

I started at a former convent near Quaker House, called Abbotsford. The Sisters of the Good Shepherd took in orphans and girls in "moral danger," and put them to work from 1863-1975. Life was hard at the convent, "draconian" according to reports made as recently as 1960. The nuns and their charges farmed, ran an industrial school and took in laundry. The kitchen often fed 1,000 people.

In contrast to the harshness of its history, the

campus is exquisite. Eleven brick buildings with gothic windows soared dramatically over acres of gardens. I lingered by trees that reminded me of catalpas, but with purple blossoms. A tall, white steeple stretched up into the sky over the stone chapel. The entire property is now a foundation dedicated to the arts. It was filled with people eating at the organic restaurant, and viewing the pond in the lower garden.

The next day I drove to the Mornington Peninsula. I found a short hike that afforded me a surprising amount of solitude given that it was Christmastime. I walked for miles along the clean beach, finding an old ferry pier, now in ruins. The water was blue and alive as the waves swept up onto the yellow sand. Our beaches in the Pacific Northwest have dark green water reflecting the omni-present greens of cedars and hemlocks. The beaches in Kuwait are so dirty that I found it difficult to want to walk along them. Construction debris was dumped along any empty beach and the water was as smooth as glass most of the time. No crashing waves to add drama to the scene. The contrast highlighted the physical and emotional drain I experienced living in the poor environmental conditions of Kuwait. In Australia, I reveled in the gorgeous blue ocean water, feeling grateful for the beauty, and lucky to have lived in such beauty for most of my life.

As I walked a bit further, I came to several groves of eerie-looking trees. There must have been a fire at some point, as all the trunks and branches were scorched black. The trees had no leaves and the ground was ash colored. It was a stark, but beautiful landscape. A little further down the trail, the scene shifted again, showing me every conceivable shade of green on the hillside above the sea. I was up high enough to find those greens reflected in the shoals under the shallow water along the shore. After months of living in all shades of sand, I breathed that green in deeply. Along the edge of the beach were incredible formations that looked as if a giant child had scooped up the sandstone and trickled it out into drippy sand castles. That night, I slept soundly and happily in my room at Quaker House.

A couple of days later I headed out on the Great Ocean Road, following the southern coast of Australia from Torquay to Allansford. I loved going at my own speed, which tends to be a little slower than most and a little faster than some. I stopped wherever I felt like it, kept going if I wanted, and generally moseyed around as I pleased. After difficult marriages and raising children, this was the first time I had traveled without having to consider anyone else's needs.

The Great Ocean Road is spectacular, with crashing waves along a wild coastline. As I was driving along, I spotted a white seagull off the left hand side of the road (the side I was driving on, still getting used to that). I glanced over again only to discover that it was a cockatiel. A huge, white, wild cockatiel just flying around in the trees! And then a flock of them. I couldn't believe my eyes. I am thrilled to see just about anything in the wild, but when it is something so exotic to me, well, what a bonus.

Soon I came to one of the sites I most wanted to see, the Twelve Apostles. The Twelve Apostles are eight free-standing sea stacks formed in layers of yellow and gray sandstone. There used to be nine, and they were called the Sow and Piglets. Renamed to encourage tourism I suppose, they became the Twelve Apostles, despite the numerical discrepancy. One, presumably Judas, collapsed and then there were eight. Their shapes twist and cavort, bending to the weathering of wind, weather and surf. They are magnificent. The waves crash up against them, spraying water up the steep cliffs nearby. I was immersed in that grace-filled joy and appreciation that washes over me in the presence of majesty.

I continued driving along the coast. One of the things I loved was viewing the trees at distance. They reminded me of Dr. Seuss trees with well-defined branches ending in round clumps of leaves. Very different from the U.S. or Kuwait. God definitely has a sense of humor. Speaking of which, my next mission was to find koala bears. I was dedicated enough to this mission that I actually stopped at a family-run zoo/tourist trap that advertised along the road. When I got out of the car the owners came out to tell me they were temporarily closed. But they knew a great (free) viewing spot.

I followed their directions and came upon more koalas than I had dared hope for. Not quite hordes, but almost. They were living in the wild, although the road along which they lived was clogged with other gawkers like me. Most of the koalas were up in the eucalyptus trees, clinging to branches almost stripped of leaves. They were little round balls of fur with fuzzy ears sticking out on either side of their heads. One crawled down to give us a show, but, wow, was it ever awkward on the ground. It was bow-legged, and seemed to err in the direction of curling into a ball rather than stretching its limbs to walk. What a treat to see it up close.

It was then time to head back to Quaker House. I passed through a couple of impossibly small towns where people sold homemade everything. Australia can be a solitary place in all its expansiveness, but solitary is familiar territory for me.

My days of exploring outside the city needed to come to an end as the job fair was approaching. I moved out of the comfort and familiarity of Quaker House, turned in the rental car and headed for a hotel in the center of Melbourne. Sitting beside the Yarra River, I shifted my attention to job seeking. I vowed to be more enthusiastic than I was during the last round of interviews. Up until I turned 50, I was offered every job I ever applied for. I spent considerable time trying to figure out the dynamics when that changed and I started getting turned down for jobs. As young people, we are always trying to appear confident, when, in fact, we are terrified at interviews. I was now completely confident in interviews; maybe that came off as arrogant or inflexible. One of my supervisors told me she was surprised I did not "sell" myself more assertively in our interview. So I would try a little salesmanship this time. I wanted to explore this international school business one more time.

The job fair process is an intense three days. The first day is spent trying to convince school administrators you have enough interesting qualities that they should interview you. I was more limited in school choices this time around because I was now 60 years old, over many schools' age limits . I hustled from table to table, briefly pitching myself, and rounded up eight interviews. I went to a few presentations by schools, and had a couple I was extremely interested in, one in South Korea and another in Cebu, the Philippines. I felt less pressure than the last time I interviewed; if I didn't find a good fit, I would go back to my job in the States.

Interviews began the next day. I spoke with the

administrators of an experientially oriented school in a planned community in South Korea. I really enjoyed the principal of the elementary school and wholeheartedly supported their hands-on style of teaching. Unfortunately, I did not have experience with the Primary Years Programme, the elementary International Baccalaureate curriculum. Next I spoke with the special education director in Cebu. We hit it off, but she was planning to hire from within. (As I write this, it is just a few weeks after the brutal typhoon ripped through the Philippines, including beautiful Cebu. This has happened to me twice. When I was graduating with my BA, I got a job in Nicaragua. I chickened out and didn't go; a massive earthquake tore through the city, destroying most of it. It is a spooky feeling to have been spared twice in this way. Maybe my philosophy of the randomness of life is wrong; maybe everything *does* happen for a reason.)

I had a couple of real possibilities, one of them in a beautiful, rural section of Thailand. The school was residential, and they wanted me to organize the after-school and weekend activities for the boarding students. Some of them were only in the first grade. I couldn't imagine six year olds living away from their families. The other was a high school position that involved developing a special education program for the school. But I was ready for something outside of the special ed world.

In between interviews, I explored downtown Melbourne. There was so much within walking distance of the hotel; a beautiful cathedral, cafes, street performers doing acrobatics using audience-held high wires. Federation Square was across the river and home to a wonderful museum of aboriginal art with its vivid colors and elegant patterns. Down the opposite direction was the Aquarium, advertising sea dragons. And truth in advertising it was. Sea dragons are related to sea horses and about the same size. They, too, have been visited by Dr. Seuss. They are yellow and flowy, and have flat, round paddles shooting randomly off their bodies. Some trailed billowy tendrils behind them. They were the most magical creatures I have ever seen.

Toward the end of the job fair, I met some wonderful administrators from a school in Bangladesh, a beautiful, poverty-stricken paradise. They were clearly a close-knit group and had a lot of fun together, which is big in my book. As they described how patient a person had to be to live there, how dysfunctional the country was, I realized for the first time that maybe I didn't want to deal with all of that again. I left the interview saying, "Well, if this doesn't work out, I can always go back to the States." I said that to a recruiter! Very bad form!

Ambivalence came into full focus for me at that moment. I hadn't realized until those words came out of my mouth that maybe I didn't want to live overseas. There were at least two jobs I knew I could have had, yet I didn't want them. I have raised my children and didn't want to raise other people's in rural Thailand. And I didn't want to continue in the special education field. I left the fair jobless, and felt just fine about it.

Chapter 26
Ya Ghafur, The Forgiving

Two Men's Gyms in My Neighborhood

So I went back to work in Kuwait. Things were a little better. I was learning that if I wanted to operate differently from everyone else, I needed to accept that I might be misunderstood; it comes with the territory. I talked with Angella, the counselor, and said that if she were willing, I would like to try to repair our relationship. After all, we had another six months to go. Angella was willing to talk, and said that she was in a different place than she had been before the holiday. Before the holiday, she had been "done." She also said, "You're not going to be here next year. Why do you care so much?" Interesting.

I still didn't have much to do, since any effort on my part was obstructed by my office mates. I managed to find a few projects to work on. Almost every staff member took me aside to tell me how much they wanted me to stay. That was very moving, and more than a little seductive. My old self would have complied in order not to disappoint, in order to save the day. But I would still have an utterly crazy system to deal with, and that was not for me. To my own surprise, I felt ready to relinquish outward action not expand it. (This somehow feels more appropriate for a person hitting age 70, not 60, but I'm often 10 years ahead in life stage issues.) It was an important milestone in my life to make decisions that were not based solely on what other people wanted from me.

I was having a wholly different type of experience at the personal level since returning from Australia. I continued to process the cracking open of my being to provide more room for the light of the Universe. The smallest of interactions frequently brought me to tears of joy.

In the book, *Be Love*, Ram Dass describes realization as living in loving awareness, an ocean of love. The realized being feels loved unconditionally and protected from harm, like an infant in the arms of a devoted mother. I wanted the rest of my life to be transmitting and receiving that loving awareness as much as possible. What else matters? What outer work could be more important?

There were a few more people I needed to forgive, notably Barb and Fayrah. So far, I had kept my distance from them. Part of me wanted to say, "I do not forgive you. You have treated me with gross disregard, and I want nothing to do with you." But there they were – and there I was. I didn't need to trust them, but I did need to forgive them. Could I forgive someone even if I remained angered by their actions? I didn't think either of them could talk things through; this was a silent forgiving, done to relieve my pain which blocked the light from coming through.

My free time was spent in reading and the occasional outing. I was learning to be a human being instead of a human doing. I couldn't quite remember why everything had seemed so urgent at home, so overwhelmingly burdensome. I followed my body's needs closely, and assimilated my learning from Australia. I was in recovery.

And I was so grateful – for everything. It felt wonderful!

The truth is that my life in Kuwait was very similar to my life at home, except that work was massively more crazy. I definitely had a Dorothy in Oz experience: "There's no place like home, there's no place like home." But what was I to do to support myself? Overseas work was probably out of the running. I needed to let the school in the U.S. know by February if I was going to return or not. Not much time to wait for other overseas options to open up.

If I went back to work in the States, the trick would be maintaining my detachment from big education issues like funding and inadequate resources for kids. When I'm looking at a room full of little faces, each with their own stories, it's a lot more difficult to detach. Yet I knew that personally I needed to be slowing down and maintaining my newfound self-acceptance. There was no question in my mind that full-time teaching in the U.S. would sap my energy beyond what I could replenish. Could I take the leap of faith and look for a job that was more manageable, but payed significantly less money?

One great thing about being in Kuwait was that I discovered how little I really needed to live comfortably. I no longer needed a house. I didn't need much in the way of material goods, though I wanted to live comfortably, not in a state of martyrdom. I began to weigh possibilities. Could I work part-time? Could I switch back to a counseling position? At least then I would be dealing with one person at a time instead of 28. Where could I live? I knew I needed to have beauty around me, and that I needed to live as economically as possible. Before I left the States I had figured if I could take home $2,000 a month in retirement, I would be fine. Might as well put that theory to the test and see if I could make it on that right now.

I began the process of talking with the principal of my old school. He was open to the idea of me working three or four days a week. Our district had always been generous about part-timers, which was unheard of, especially in elementary schools. "Which would you rather do, work three or four days?" he asked me. Oh, no, I had to assess my own needs and desires; not my strong suit. I bit the bullet, surrounded myself with the knowledge that I would be OK (I was pretty sure) and said three days only. Much to my surprise, he was pleased; three days could provide him with a lot of flexibility. We began talking about how to best use my skill set the following year. I relaxed into the decision, feeling settled and calm, with only a splash of uncertainty.

Accusations and ridiculous things continued to happen at work, but these were just more of the same. I stopped mentioning every incident in my emails home. It had become boring and expected. Not that life was easy; it was extremely stressful, but the element of surprise and shock had worn off. Besides, there was a two-week holiday coming up in February. We had extensive holidays, and I loved traveling at off-peak vacation times.

I started planning my next adventure. I designed a great itinerary starting in Jordan and traveling to Petra. I had never heard of Petra before coming to Kuwait, but movie buffs will know it as the location of an exciting scene from the first Indiana Jones movie, *Raiders of the Lost Ark*. If that's too archaic of a reference, President Obama visited there shortly after I did. I would explore Petra, travel to the southern tip of Jordan where I could snorkel, and then take a ferry to Egypt. Starting in the Valley of the Kings I could proceed northward to the Pyramids to end my trip. I'd always wanted to see the antiquities in Egypt – I had plans as a child to be an archaeologist. I was excited.

But life interfered, as it has a habit of doing. Demonstrations were spreading through Egypt and my travel agent in Kuwait could not contact her colleagues to book accommodations for me. If arrangements had been possible, I'm sure I could have made the trip safely. The demonstrations were confined to a couple of small areas that could be avoided. In fact, one of the Shamiya teachers spent the holidays there and encountered no difficulties. Worrying about the demonstrations would be referred to as the "CNN effect," according to the world of international schools. We were cautioned against it.

Without a place to stay in Egypt, I switched to Plan B. I decided to go to Turkey after Jordan. Nora, my dear friend back home and great supporter of my journey of the spirit, suggested I look at a travel website from a hometown boy. I came across a YouTube video of Mimi, a travel guide, describing the huge public toilet in Ephesus, the largest excavated Roman ruin. It boasted a spot for an entire orchestra to play, thereby blocking out the sounds of so many people answering the call of nature at one time. I was hooked and prepared to take off for Jordan and Turkey. Alone again, but this time with guides. Having a guide seemed like an enormous luxury, and certainly a breach of my family's code of not appearing to be tourists, even when we were tourists. Given the language barriers I was about to encounter, a guide was definitely in order. And the truth is I want to see the same things everyone else wants to see. *Oooh, I'm letting go of* Differentness.

Chapter 27

Ya Majid, The All Glorious, The Majesty

A Djinn Block, Petra, Jordan

Just being in Jordan was a treat. People were smiling there, and nice to stray cats. In Kuwait, some of our students tossed a kitten back and forth until it died. When I saw Jordanian faces wreathed in smiles, it reminded me of how few I saw in Kuwait. All that wealth, and no smiles.

Unlike Kuwait, Jordan has geography, and trees! Olive trees everywhere! I was enchanted by the intersection of different religions at each sacred site. Christians and Muslims have lived together peacefully in Jordan for centuries. The relationship with Jews is more complicated, although the authentic teachings of Islam emphasize respect for all people who believe in one God.

Not being a city person, I spent very little time in

Amman, the capital. I did have a chance to see the remains of an enormous Roman amphitheater. Spectacular and majestic. Then I headed to Mount Nebo which overlooks the Jordan Valley. This was the spot from which Moses saw the Promised Land, but was told by God that he would never go there. God had instructed Moses to tap gently on a rock to produce a spring. Instead, Moses struck in anger. Not going to the Promised Land was the result. That spring still flows today and ordinary people go there with plastic jugs to collect their drinking water.

Mount Nebo is one of the places where the Virgin Mary lived after the Crucifixion. There were not many archaeological artifacts of that time, although there was a lot of restoration work being done. Incredible Byzantine mosaics, with unbelievably complex and rich designs, were displayed outdoors under a shade. I marveled at the craftsmanship that went into works of art made of tiles a quarter inch square.

I drove around the Dead Sea and could see Israel from where I was. It was too cold to get in and float, but I did see salt crystals with the most beautiful and delicate patterns forming at the edge of the water. Unfortunately, the Dead Sea is shrinking three feet per year because the cosmetic industry uses up the minerals at a prodigious rate. Potash and other minerals are also removed for industrial purposes. Up on a hill on the other side of the road stood the pillar of salt that had once been Lot's wife. The contrast between old and new was mind-boggling.

Next on my itinerary were two castles built by the Crusaders. Initially, I was excited to see my very first castle. Once I got there, however, I looked at them from the point of view of Middle Easterners, which precluded any romanticization. The Crusades were a plague to the people in the Middle East. Seen as obstacles to the "Quest" to wrench Jerusalem from Islamic rule, Muslims were flung into the castles' numerous torture chambers. All in the name of money and power. The structures themselves were amazing, and I wondered at the ability to build in the absence of today's tools.

Seeing things that I'd heard about all my life, that happened over 2,000 years ago, transformed me in a subtle way. I began to understand how history unfolded in very straight-forward terms. My brother once said he couldn't comprehend a beaver dam until he saw one on a lake. I know I could *not* figure out locks in canals until I watched a real boat go through a real lock. Jordan provided me with similar insight into human beings, and the growth of civilization during ancient times. The harsh heat and pervasive sand helped me understand why people were always washing Jesus' feet, and anointing them with oil. The olive branch was brought back to Noah on the Ark from one of the extensive groves that still blanket the landscape today. What seemed exotic to me in the States was simply logical in the land of olives.

Petra is the absolute gem of Jordan. Sometimes when I visit a place I've read about, I'm disappointed; it's not as impressive as I expect without filtered camera shots. Petra, however, does not disappoint. If anything, it is even more vivid in person than in photos. I remember wondering how on earth anyone ever found this surreal landscape tucked into a chasm in the ground.

The deeper I went into the site, the more everything made sense. Petra was discovered during the time when the Nabateans were nomadic. They moved constantly trying to find just a bit of vegetation and just enough water to keep their sheep alive. They had to find areas that were not too hot in the summer or too cold in the winter. Although there is more vegetation in Jordan than in Kuwait, it is still sparse.

So on one such ordinary excursion, I imagine, someone must have stumbled into Petra. They discovered, just as I did, a myriad of stones, golden, rose, black, all layered next to each other on the ground and in the rock faces. A deep gorge leads into the site, flanked by an aqueduct carved into the sides of the canyons to transport water to the dwellings. It is so awe-inspiring that people of many different traditions immediately recognized it as a sacred place.

One of the first man-made things I came upon were huge, rectangular blocks, Djinn Blocks. These massive carved stones were believed to entrap the Djinns (as in Genies). It's important to keep those Djinns out of mischief; they cannot be relied upon to work for the greater good. For Sufis, they are beings that live on the plane of pure thought, thought with no object. It is a place that all humans descend through on their way to earth. After death, we ascend back through the Djinn plane as we reunify with the Divine. Some theorize that the Djinn Blocks are tombs or representations of Nabatean gods.

Further into the gorge are betels carved into the walls. They look like picture frames, the reliefs they framed now almost completely worn away. Mausoleums, and reliefs of life-size camels in a caravan line the pathway through the gorge. The camels' feet are as big as flattened cantaloupes.

After about a mile, the long, narrow chasm opens without warning onto the Treasury. Its massive facade is carved out of a rose-red cliff, though the sunlight can cast it golden. The Treasury looks like a Greek or Roman temple, complete with plastic-helmeted Centurions on site for photo ops. Past this opulent carving, I roamed through a long valley full of modest caves and spectacular mausoleums. Most of the facades were tributes to important leaders of the time. One of the things I could not figure out is how they have survived for so long. If you pick up a red rock from the ground, it crumbles in your hand like sandstone. I could see how easily it could be carved, but it is so fragile; how has it not all eroded away?

I walked for seven hours, enthralled, enchanted. My body started to protest, but I simply could not stop.

The valley beyond the gorge is filled with Bedouins, selling wares and offering rides on camels, horses and mules. If Johnny Depp was attractive in *Pirates of the Caribbean*, imagine a valley filled with Jack Sparrows. Their hair is dark and long, they outline their eyes with kohl and dress like gypsies. Some of them live part of the year in the caves of Petra and they also have a village not far from the entrance. Most gorgeous men I have ever seen.

Many offered to give me their cell phone number so I could call them when I was lonely. They offered to take me to their cave or their village. Most of all they offered to sell me things. "Make my day," the little ones say to enhance their marketing. At the same time, they are proud, and independent, and I didn't see the downtrodden expressions I saw on the faces of the overworked Indians and Filipinos in Kuwait.

As I traveled further into the valley, Roman colonnaded streets appeared, Byzantine mozaics, churches with baptismal fonts, temples, green marble columns from Egypt. As her children squabbled beside her, a Bedouin woman sold me an ancient coin she had found on the site. Finally I reached the end of the valley and sat to have something to drink. My knees ached, and I felt that good tired you get when you've pushed yourself physically. I had been planning to come back the next day, but realized my body was worn out. I wouldn't be able to return.

Unfortunately, I hadn't seen the Monastery. People along the path said I really needed to see the Monastery; only 800 stone steps more. On the spur of the moment, after refusing offers all day long, I decided to hire a mule to take me up. It was quite late, and most of the Bedouin were packing up, but there were still a few mules around.

My history with riding is not a proud one. My uncle had horses, and when I was 21 he decided I should learn to ride, bareback. I grew up a city-slicker, and had not yet become a country person. So it was scary. Uncle Wyatt lived in the countryside of upstate New York, and he brought a small pony out onto his driveway; my feet almost reached the ground as I sat on her. She took one step forward, I stayed exactly where I was, falling straight to the ground.

On another visit, he decided I should try with a saddle; no pony this time, a real horse. I had no idea how big a horse was! My young cousins rode like the wind, and took off through the corn-fields. My horse was very clear I had no idea what I was doing, and flew off after them. Somehow I managed to hang on.

Since then, I've frequently said that I was more confident now, and could probably be the one in control of a horseback ride. Theories are beautiful things, and this one was almost legitimate. But now I was putting it to the test. I got on the mule, not nearly as big as a horse, and he immediately tried to buck me off. The Bedouin saved me, grabbing the mule's halter, a short link chain. Because I have little T-rex arms, it was hard for me to hold the short chain without choking the mule, which was distressing for both of us.

We started up the steep, incredibly beautiful stone stairway to the Monastery. The Bedouin told me to lean forward going uphill, and soon I could follow the rhythm of the mule. He was shod and sometimes his feet slipped on the smooth stone, sometimes right next to a long, steep drop-off. Very scary. Sometimes the mule let me know it was quitting time, and tried to scrape me off against the side of the cliff. But we persevered and reached the furthest point to which the mule could go. Despite painful knees, I had to traverse the last steep bit on foot. When I came into the opening from the path, the sight was truly unbelievable. The Monastery was the largest of all the carvings, 160 stories high. Up on top of one of the highest columns, a young Bedouin man danced gracefully, calling down to us to join him. The rock formations were astounding; the Monastery was worth the trip.

I got better at riding on the way down. I had to lean backwards under a natural stone arch and again my short arms were a problem. Plus I had a backpack on and could only flatten out so much. I hoped I wouldn't scrape my face off. When we got down I decided to pay extra to ride out to the entrance. The Bedouin asked, "You have horse at home?"

185

"No," I said.

"Why not?"

"No money."

"No money, honey." We rode as far as the Treasury; after that, the horsemen had the monopoly, so I walked the rest of the way out. I could not believe I was in Petra, seeing these incredible sites! And this was only the beginning. Turkey awaited.

Chapter 28

Ya Karim, The Generous

Cappadocia, Turkey

After the grandeur of Petra, I flew from Amman to Istanbul, a short flight into a completely different world. Driving from the airport to the old city is the only nice airport drive I've ever taken. No industrial areas, just the Bosphorus, ancient Roman walls and beautiful flower gardens, even in February. The flowers were planted in serifs and gentle curves; it was beautiful.

Flowers are important to Turks. To my surprise, Holland is not where tulips originated. The Dutch found them in what is now Turkey ... growing wild with tiny, delicate, pointed petals. They are an omnipresent motif throughout Turkey.

Istanbul is enormous; the taxi turned off a large arterial and drove me to a small hotel in the middle of the old part of the city. The streets were steep and narrow, and still paved with paving stones. They twisted and turned, and although I have a good sense of direction, I got lost the second time I went out walking. Different layers of civilization literally sit on top of each other throughout Istanbul and other parts of Turkey.

The first known human settlement in Anatolia was near Catalhoyuk, and dates back to approximately 6500 BCE. Turkey has been home to no less than eleven empires (Hittite, Trojan, Phrygian – Midas' kingdom, Lycian and Lydian whose people built the Temple of Artemis, Persian, Roman, Byzantine Turk, Seljuk, Ottoman Empires). The influences of these highly developed cultures are apparent everywhere in the architecture and art. Istanbul is definitely the place to go for incredible mosques, churches, and Roman remains such as the Hippodrome. Here chariots raced around symbols of all parts of the Roman empire, including Egypt. An Egyptian obelisk is mounted on several sets of blocks to allow flexibility during earthquakes. That long ago, people had the technology to prevent damage, using basically the same techniques that are considered state of the art today. We're not so smart after all.

Mimi, my guide, picked me up on my second day in Turkey. She was extremely knowledgeable and used her tours to make history come alive. Her commentary links all of us to the same set of human desires, to build a better life for ourselves and our children. It was just the two of us, and I couldn't have been in better hands. Her daughter, Avril, had told me I would leave Turkey with a friend for life.

We saw the famous Blue Mosque, Aya Sofia, the Grand Bazaar, Topkapi Palace, and more. All were incredible pieces of architecture, art and craft. I particularly loved the Basilica Cistern, another amazing feat of engineering. Managing water is vital to any city's ability to survive. But the Basilica Cistern did not resemble my Grandmother Minnie's back in Sioux City, Iowa. Grandma Minnie's cistern was kind of like a concrete cave in one part of her basement. The Basilica Cistern is underground, too, but built with leftover columns and carvings from other eras. Poor Medusa is lying on her side or standing on her head at the bottom of support columns. As a kid, I was fascinated by the different types of columns – Corinthian, Ionian, Doric; I loved Greek myths and Medusa often stood out in my imagination. In Turkey, she is not the monster portrayed in the myths I read, but is considered a protector. The blue glass eye that I have at home, like ones all over Turkey, is a symbol of her protective eye, not the blue of Alexander the Great's as I had once been told.

A city person could not find a better city to explore. The food is great, the jewels on display outrageous, and in February, street vendors sell a wonderful hot drink with milk and orchid root, that even I, spurner of coffee and tea, loved. There were roasted chestnuts being sold from handcarts and every kind of market imaginable.

The second day in Turkey, Mimi asked me what my experience in Kuwait had been like. It was hard to answer that question as I would not have believed my own story six months earlier. I never imagined people would act with such ruthless aggression. And I hate to appear/be negative or culturally intolerant. I allowed as how it had been quite challenging, and gave a few minor examples of what it was like. I told her we had fingerprint machines we used to punch in and out every day, and that if we took a single sick day we had to produce a doctor's excuse. (There's a guy who sits in the basement of the hospital giving out sick leave forms. You tell him you have a stomachache and he gives you a note citing respiratory problems.)

She immediately said, "You have to get out of that prison." Mimi is not one to mince words. "I have an apartment above my office in Kusadasi; I'll show it to you and if you like it, you can stay there for as long as you want." This was like something straight out of a movie! And shocking to my pathologically independent soul, which often has trouble asking for help even once I finally realize I need it. My friend, Allie, tells me, "There is help out there, Zanne, but you do have to ask for it."

Jalaluddin Rumi affirms, "You need so much more Grace than you realize." Going it alone had become such a pattern in my life, that I was completely bowled over by this overwhelmingly generous offer from an absolute stranger. And I recognized how badly I wanted to leave the painful and unhealthy situation in Kuwait.

So I thought about it. For two days I was so stunned by the offer that I didn't know what to say to Mimi. Finally, on the third day, I apologized for what might have appeared to be nonchalance about her proposal. I explained how overcome with emotion and gratitude I was. She replied that she would arrange some kind of job for me so I could buy groceries. Really her motivation was to put me at ease so I wouldn't feel like a freeloader or a stray cat she had picked up. She said that anyone in Turkey would offer this kind of help. Really? I wasn't so sure about that. My heart lifted; the plan felt right to me. So I thought about it some more.

190

Meanwhile, we had flown into the heart of Anatolia to Cappadocia. Cappadocia is located in a large valley situated between two volcanic mountains. Eruptions had filled the valley with soft rock called tuff, creating rock formations that reminded me of Dr. Seuss' houses in Who-ville. I had seen photos online of these fairy chimneys and homes, and imagined they existed in a small area. Instead they range around in a region 40,000 miles square.

The inhabitants of the area discovered that tuff was very easy to carve. Once the rock came into contact with air, it hardened. They began hollowing holes into these magical formations just large enough for one person to crawl through. Next, carving from within began, and houses, monasteries and churches were created within these formations. Where the carvings of Petra were ornamental, the carvings in Cappodocia represent a beautiful union between art and habitat.

The structures go on and on. Many are decorated with stunning frescoes, often depicting the life of Jesus. I always imagined frescoes as muted colors, earth tones. They are earth tones, but none of this warm brown or yellow that I thought of as natural dyes in the U.S. The colors remain brilliant today … ruby reds, cobalt blues.

One thing I absolutely love about Turkey is its long history of different religions and cultures layered side by side in the architecture and history. Although this area had been part of the Persian Empire with its Islamic tradition, some of the people of Cappodocia embraced early Christianity. It is thought that Jesus' disciples brought their ministry to the area soon after the Resurrection. The teachings took hold quickly, hence the monastery and artwork commemorating Christ's life. The monastery was conceived of as a place of education rather than retreat. It is filled with classrooms and chapels where the monks taught anyone who was interested; a place that had been filled with life. There is a sacred feel to each of these fantastical, whimsical structures.

The Greeks and Romans held sway over Turkey as well, and were concerned about the challenge to their power inherent in Christianity. They began to raid Cappodocia. The Christians went underground, literally. They carved huge, subterranean tuff cities, with zigzagging chimneys. The chimneys took so many turns that no one at the surface could spot the smoke from their fires. Large numbers of people would sometimes have to stay hidden for months. Seeing the actual conditions simply cannot compare to a mental concept of persecution.

Entrances were hidden and the forethought that went into the planning is unbelievable. There were birthing areas, altars, wine-making facilities. Mimi and I imagined that living in darkness, feeling the way, crawling through steep, winding passages, probably required a lot of fortification. I'm sure the wine was not wasted.

Not too far away is Konya, the home of the great Sufi, Jalaluddin Rumi. As we approached Konya, Mimi asked me when I had first learned about the Sufis. It had been about 37 years, which surprised her. Most Westerners have only become aware of him recently as translations of his poetry were widely published and read. We entered a Caravanserai, a place where caravans rested at the end of the Silk Road. Here we would see the Whirling Dervishes practice in the lamplight. It was cold, and Mimi and I went into an old camel stall to talk.

She asked again why I was so interested in the Sufis. My uncertainty about how Sufism might be viewed resurfaced. I wasn't sure where to begin or how much to share.

Finally, I threw caution to the winds, and told Mimi that I had joined the Chisti Order of the Sufis 37 years ago. The Chisti order is not the order of Rumi; his followers are Mevlevi. Both seek ecstasy and union with the One Being; the Chistis use sound to attune to the Divine Qualities of the Beloved, while the Mevlevis whirl and become one with the music of the spheres. Mimi revealed that she was born and raised a Sufi, and sees Sufism as a way of life. No wonder I felt such a bond with her. I loved her ability to juxtapose strong opinions with absolute lack of judgment. Reconciling the irreconciliables defines my practice of Sufism, though I have not mastered it as well as Mimi has.

We entered the hall where the Mevlevi Sufis whirl to witness this aesthetic and spiritual joy. The Dervishes wear tall felt hats that represent their tombstones. "Die before death and resurrect now." The movement begins with arms folded into the chest, symbolizing union; as they whirl, their arms extend, one reaching toward the heavens, the other toward the earth. Eventually, they return to the posture of total absorption in the Divine. I was ecstatically absorbed as well.

But I also felt discomfort ... the same discomfort I feel when Madeline, my Choctaw sister-in-law, takes me to see Indian ceremonies. (She prefers "Indian" to "Native American.") We once attended an all night healing ceremony during a period of time when I sorely needed healing. I struggled, not wanting to diminish the ceremony, the sacredness, by participating as audience to a performance. Perhaps the Indian dancers and the whirling Dervishes have come to terms with this tension.

The last leg of the journey was to Kusadasi on the Aegean Sea, near Ephesus. Ephesus is the largest Greco-Roman excavation in the world, and another absolute marvel of ancient sophistication. It covered a much larger area than I imagined and had a population of 250,000. About 85 percent of the city remains to be unearthed. The homes of the wealthy were three stories high, had running water, indoor toilets and heat. The walls were covered in beautiful frescoes depicting important myths, and the enormous rooms were "carpeted" with intricate mosaics that mimicked the patterns and borders of traditional carpets. There is one avenue lined with the remains of various shops. The city and the nearby Temple of Artemis were both considered among the Seven Wonders of the Ancient World.

The famous Celsus Library, built in 124 CE, stands at the foot of one of the main avenues in Ephesus. At one time it held 12,000 papyrus scrolls. Papyrus looks a lot like the impenetrable clumps of pampas grass in the Pacific Northwest. The entrance is guarded by statues representing wisdom, goodness, judgment, knowledge, and by Nike, the winged angel of victory. Stray cats roam around getting into tourists' photographs. The Turks are quite loving to their strays, but the tourists are not. The day I was there, a man ruthlessly threw the cats out of the way of his photo. It was brutal; Mimi was appalled.

Christian history played out in Ephesus during the early '50s CE. There are those who believe that Paul wrote the Epistle to the Ephesians while held in prison there. He had a beef with the artisans selling images of Artemis, whose temple stood nearby. The house of

Mary, believed to be Mary's last home on this earth, is also close to Ephesus. John is purported to have brought Mary to this small stone structure to live out her days. People write their prayers on scraps of paper and insert them into a wire mesh wall. The wall replaced the tradition of tying notes to branches and shrubs surrounding the humble stone cottage. There is an atmosphere of great peace and harmony in that place. I was lucky to be there at a time when few people were around.

Mary figures strongly in my discovery of the spiritual world; when I was beginning Sufi practices back in my twenties, I had a vision of Mary one night. I found that strange; I didn't have a lot of images or concepts of Her after growing up in an atheistic household. And I am the least visual person I know, yet there she was, as clear as day, smiling at me and beckoning me into her arms. This was very powerful to me as I was in a period of trying to prove my worthiness to myself and anyone else who would listen. I had been a grossly neglected child. I did not feel, nor would I for a very long time, as though I deserved love and care from anyone, let alone the Virgin Mary.

Oh, it was just a dream, some might say. My Sufi teacher did not even acknowledge the experience when I described it to her. Sufis, wisely, don't like to get hung up on phenomenology, and go chasing after sensation. That tends to distract people from the real work of meditation, and the real truth of living with love and compassion. My sense is that the lack of response was meant as a protection against developing pride in my "spiritual progress."

Later, after my mother died, I had another vision of Mary with my mother standing beside her. As I gratefully saw them welcoming me once again into their arms, my mother melded into the form of Mary. What a comfort for the newly motherless child I was. I felt a sense of peacefulness and love as I entered the stone house near Ephesus. I could feel the warmth of Mary's presence in my heart. I learned later that Mary was given the role of healer, one of the reasons She is so revered in the Catholic Church. She certainly fulfills this role in my life.

Kusadasi is Mimi's home; I was able to see her office, the apartment above it that she had offered me, her home and her farm. I met the "family" she has assembled; there is an easy companionship amongst them, although Mimi is clearly at the center and clearly in charge. As I watched their closeness I was torn by wanting to be a part of that, and at the same time afraid I might not fit in. I suspected they didn't care, and would be more than happy to let me be a hermit, but the discomfort surfaced anyway. Did I have what it takes to live in close community like that?

When I left Turkey, I was not entirely certain whether to take Mimi up on her generous offer.

Chapter 29

Ya Khabir, The Reality Knower

A Hotel in Sri Lanka

It was the beginning of March when I returned to Kuwait from Turkey. I had this nagging feeling that I ought to try one more time to straighten things out at work. I am either highly conscientious or a glutton for punishment. The outrageous stories continued on a daily basis, but it seemed unnecessary to keep documenting same craziness, different day. The last two incidents, however, were very serious, and involved possible physical abuse of students by staff. This is where I have to draw the line. Spew all the vitriol you like, but do not endanger kids on my watch.

Angella, the counselor who reported these abuses to me, refused to divulge the details I needed to go to the superintendent. She was on Barb's side, and would only talk to Barb, who had been out sick for several days. With another holiday fast approaching, I repeatedly tried to get the information I needed, but

Angella refused. Then the holiday was upon us. I was spitting nails by then. Something had to change.

Another fact kept intruding on my mind; the majority of students would stop attending school in May and June. Although school continued through June, the weather is so hot that most families pull their kids out, and travel to a more moderate climate. I realized that meant I would have to spend the last two months of work helping the school become reaccredited as an international school, a process in which I did not want to participate. In my opinion, the school did not merit reaccreditation. It quickly became obvious to me that I needed to leave Kuwait for my own sanity and to preserve my sense of ethics. Again, I was stunned that Ms. UberResponsible was making a decision to break a contract. No small thing.

I worked the numbers and figured that if I stayed at Shamiya School two more months, I would have enough money to get through until my first paycheck in the U.S. at the end of the following September. I wrote Mimi, accepting her offer of asylum, and bought a ticket to Turkey departing April 29.

My time in Kuwait was growing short, which was good because the lousy air quality wreaked havoc with my stomach and ears. I felt nauseous and kept getting ear infections. I had pediatric tubes in my ears creating holes through my eardrums. The constant blowing sand was a real hazard. We had one more holiday coming up, and my friend, Mary, and I decided to go to Sri Lanka for five days. After that I would have two more weeks at school, followed by the much anticipated flight to Turkey.

I wanted to stay out of the U.S. until July 13 so I

wouldn't have to pay taxes on my overseas income, and then I'd be on a plane that very day back to the Pacific Northwest. I would go back to Chimacum, but work only three days a week. I was looking forward to slowing down, being with friends and family, and enjoying the beauty in this life. Other people had been "the sticks God beat me with," as the Dervishes say.

The upside of all the craziness lay in the enormous chunks of ego calving off my being. Surprising realizations of the ways I misunderstood myself and my relationships with others surfaced. I saw now the unavoidable truth of how my thoughts had influenced my dealings back in the States. Although I was tactful and respectful in my communication, I recognized how much critical thinking went on in my mind; critical thinking that maintained my *Differentness* and, therefore, my own sense of superiority. People intuited this and were rightfully put off by it. I now saw how ordinary I was and how glad I was to be ordinary. No megalomaniacal sense that I was the one who would save Shamiya School, the American public schools or anything else. I was ready finally to accept the whole trove of grace that I previously had no idea I so desperately needed. I felt real joy in the emptiness of self that I had discovered. I was ready to let go of the reins and ride where the Universe led me. "Here I am, God, take me," I said to myself. (Out of habit, I ducked.) The ocean takes care of each wave. I gave up my ambitions to be the ocean and practiced being grateful to be a wave.

During all this, I maintained my commitment to the staff and students with whom I was working. Although I did not want to help the school become accredited, I did want to lay in some stores for the good people that would be working there the following year. I spent a lot of energy researching materials that were appropriate for the broad range of abilities in our student population. I made sure there were hands-on materials for our concrete thinkers, and that programs were research-based if not research-proven.

I also facilitated the alignment of the entire curriculum, grades 1-12 within the Special Needs Department. This would eliminate the sense of flying by the seat of the pants that teachers had to endure. It also paved the way for students to be learning new things each year instead of repeating the same activities 12 years in a row. No more would every student classify living and non-living things for 12 years in a row. We taught staff how to differentiate instruction, exposing students to all kinds of information in a format that worked for them despite their varying abilities.

We tackled the fact that our most intellectually disabled students were still being taught letter sounds and names in the 12th grade. They did not even know what the purpose of sounds was; there was no connection for them between their tasks and the goal of reading. They tried to do well because, like all of us, they cared about being competent and pleasing the adults who were their primary connection to life and learning. These kids needed and deserved a life skills curriculum that teaches them how to care for themselves, cook, engage in recreational activities and drive. To that end, we designed a life skills room and drew up a list of equipment needed to give students the actual experience of learning daily living activities. We ordered books to guide a comprehensive curriculum and talked about how to generate "jobs" within the school community for our students. (What I didn't have time to do was canvas parents to see what they wanted their children to be able to do independently.

On another front, I introduced the staff to the difficulties students have with sensory integration. These students are legion within the special education population. They tend to be over-sensitive to touch, noise, smells and other people. They are easily distracted, crave movement, can be aggressive and easily overwhelmed. They typically are clumsy and have poor fine and gross motor skills. All of this is due to a poorly understood neurological glitch that interferes with a person interpreting the signals from their own sensory system accurately. Occupational therapists have found ways to help folks soothe themselves, and increase their attention by providing movement in a form that doesn't interfere with concentration (using large exercise balls as chairs, for example). There are many ways to counteract other sensory challenges that interfere with learning. So we ordered some items that would help kids regulate sensory input in a way that would increase their success at school.

With a sense of accomplishment at the completion of these projects, I headed away from the desert to the tropics with Mary. Sri Lanka's heat and humidity represent the anti-Kuwait. There were trees and flowers in bloom everywhere. It was gorgeous!

The cities are extremely busy and densely populated. I had been persuaded not to rent a car there, and was well-advised. Although most of the roads we drove on were two lanes only, there was always at least one other ad hoc "lane" created. In Kuwait, car horns sounded constantly in an angry, impatient sort of way. In Sri Lanka, they sounded constantly, but more as a form of communication. The cars, *tuk tuks* and trucks beep their horns to let everyone else know what they are doing, almost like a turn signal. Toot, I'm passing you. Toot, you're going to slow. Toot, I'm turning. Toot, I'm coming at you head-on and expect you to yield. And they do, not as quickly as I would have been comfortable with, but somehow it worked.

Because many people cannot afford cars, there are lots of scooters, mopeds and motorcycles. And there was one elephant being ridden down the road in Colombo. *Tuk tuks* serve as taxis and are basically three-wheeled scooters. Che Guevara visited here and many of the *tuk tuks* have references to him displayed on their vehicles. Bob Marley is another favorite. The "bumper stickers" seemed quite socialistic. Motorcycles and bikes also carry passengers; as many as four or five. The adults wear helmets, but the babies are carried in their mothers' arms. We didn't see any women driving any kind of vehicle, although the traditional culture was rooted in matriarchy. Mother Earth was the guiding light until wars and occupation finally displaced her.

The currency in Sri Lanka is rupees, so we paid 10,000 rupees for the taxi from the airport. I felt rich carrying around wads of 2,000 rupee bills. But I had a really hard time mentally converting that, and often had very little idea of how much I was spending. It was easier in other countries for some reason; maybe because the numbers were smaller. How many zeroes is that? And, of course, my exceptionally poor mental math skills are well known.

We stayed at a beautiful beach resort that Mary had been to before. Ocean view, fish pond, in-pool bar, the whole bit. The surf pounded the shore, and the water was warm as a bathtub. The sand was truly golden with other layers that were rose and lavender colored. After a walk on the beach, my feet stayed purple for days. Sri Lankans selling sarongs, carvings, and shells were scattered along the beach. There were deformed beggars and a guy with a spider monkey on a leash. (The monkeys are cute, but very bold.) And fishing boats, now made of fiberglass, but only about a foot wide; the outriggers still formed from tree branches. The seafood was amazing; shrimp like I could not believe.

Although the distances to other places were not huge, the travel times were, so Mary and I didn't get to see much more than our little corner of the country. We did take one day trip and drove through the areas hit by the tsunami in 2004. Many people were still rebuilding. One man told me that few people would swim in the ocean anymore because the tsunami had been so terrifying.

Most of the houses did not have glass windows; some people lived in nice little homes, others in tents. It still seems to me that being poor in the country offers a bit better quality of life, but how much of that opinion is romanticization I can't tell. At least there is space and beauty around. And most people seemed cheerful and friendly. Kuwait seemed such an unhappy place in comparison.

We stopped at a gem "mine" which was really just a rectangular hole dug down into the sand and supported with woven palm fronds. It was very primitive; still no OSHA! A young guy went down the main hole and into a small tunnel to dig. The sand was then put through sieves by hand, like panning for gold. The particular mine we saw was collecting moon stones. They cut and polished the stones there, and had a large showroom.

We also checked out a demonstration plot of Ayurvedic herbs that was staffed by young men studying Ayurvedic practice. The training takes twelve years. Everywhere you go in Sri Lanka you find Ayurvedic clinics and spas.

We drove (no, we were driven) to an old fort called Galle, pronounced Gaul. This area was settled by Portuguese and Dutch trading companies. Sri Lanka continues to be a big producer of spices and rubber. The architecture of Galle was quintessential colonial, with wide porches, ceiling fans and shuttered windows. We were quite the oddity around town, usually being the only two white people in sight.

We would have liked to go to Kandy an ancient fortress built up on a mesa rising out of the jungle. It is the site of the relic of Buddha's tooth. I also wanted to visit a wildlife preserve to see more elephants and wild cats. Unfortunately, we did not have time to do these things. I guess I'll have to go back.

Sri Lanka is a true spiritual crossroads. The longitudinal axis that runs through the Tibetan Buddhists' center in the Himalayas also runs through a small town in Sri Lanka. It was home to a famous Sufi, who inspired Coleman Barks to translate Jalaluddin Rumi's poetry. There are ceremonies in this town that involve being hung by cords strung through the skin on hooks, and fire walking. I was not disappointed to miss those experiences.

I have always been reluctant to visit India, thinking it would be too much for me to cope with emotionally. After the traffic, the beggars, the poverty of Sri Lanka, I confirmed my reluctance. I don't know what to do in the face of so much need. My white privilege allows me to avoid it.

The majority of people at the hotel were Russian. I was the first American the employees had ever met. The Russians burned terribly in the sun and it was a shock to see thong bikinis after living amongst *abayas*. I would nod and smile, but usually they didn't respond. I guess the etiquette at a resort is different than backpackers' etiquette. I think we should all adopt backpackers' etiquette. Say hello, smile and leave the campsite better than you found it; not a bad code to live by.

It was difficult to go back to the desert. My friend, Harper, had gone to Thailand when I was in Sri Lanka. She is wild about animals and went to a small elephant refuge. An Australian woman and her Thai husband started the refuge on his family's farmland. Running the place was dangerous business. Farmers want to shoot the elephants when they destroy their crops; the *mahouts* (elephant keepers) want to work them into the ground, giving rides to tourists. So basically this couple goes to them and offers to take the old, the sick or the marauders into their care. Feeding elephants is a serious undertaking. One way they raise money is by having guests like Harper, who is now sure that this will be her life a few years down the road.

When I returned to Shamiya School, I met with the superintendent, detailing how Angella had withheld information on possible student abuse before the holiday. "This kind of obstructionism is just too much," I said. "I can't accomplish anything under these conditions. I want to be transferred to the elementary department." I had good relationships with the principal and learning support supervisor there, and they would have happily used my skills to their advantage. Mr.

Khaled refused to transfer me. There's a surprise.

Instead, we had more meetings, a.k.a. confrontations, with the individuals involved. Basically, they were told to stop hating me; like that was going to work. Which it didn't. It just cemented people in their points of view, the needs of students unimportant in the face of their own power games.

I still didn't have enough to do to keep busy at work. It drives me crazy to just put in time or try to look busy. My relationships with the people in my immediate office remained icy. I missed the beauty of home and the other places I'd visited. One more week, and then I would leave. It began to get surreal; only two people knew I was leaving. I was now at the stage where people were asking me to do things I knew I wouldn't be around to complete.

I contemplated telling the superintendent my plans, and explaining that I had done all the heavy lifting the department required to move ahead. Now I needed to leave and take care of the physical injuries I incurred in the line of duty at school. A doctor told me several discs in my neck were compressed, probably the result of preventing two large students from running away. Three months after the incident my arm was still not healing; the doctor suggested neck surgery. This was not what I wanted to hear. I had expected to go in and ask for a steroid shot and then be on my way. There wasn't really anything to be done about it. I would like to blame the school for this – it can be caused by poor ergonomics at the computer, which I definitely had, and by accidents. But it can also be caused by a lifetime of heavy physical work, which I also had, and general wear and tear. I suspect the discomforts of Kuwait may have brought it on earlier than otherwise, but who really knows.

I even fantasized that if I explained the situation to Mr. Khaled, the school might pay me the rest of my annual salary because I had been such a good worker. I was not comfortable just disappearing, and it would have felt better to me to be aboveboard. I got some encouragement in that vein watching a young couple who were expecting a baby. The physical environment was making the woman very sick; "Essentially," the doctor told her, "you are allergic to Kuwait." The school responded really well to their situation and told the couple to do what they needed to do for the health of their baby …

For a few weeks. Then the woman was sent back to work. It was unclear when she would be allowed to leave the country. And her husband was to finish out the year, regardless of what happened with his wife and child. It became clear, once again, that I could not trust the administrators to pay me even for the time I had worked if (or when) they got angry. The plan was to collect my April paycheck and hightail it out of there; in the middle of the night, without telling anyone. Such an odd plan for someone who has always been so compliant. I couldn't wait.

Chapter 30

Ya Mudhill, The Disgracer, The Dishonorer

Column Fragments, Ephesus, Turkey

In the middle of the night on April 24, 2013, I left Kuwait. I slipped a letter under the door of a neighbor explaining my disappearance to the staff:

> Dear friends,
>
> I am writing to let you know that I
> have left Kuwait. I feel I have
> contributed as much as I can to
> Shamiya School this year; the most
> important tasks are done. Leaving you
> all is hard; I will carry a little
> piece of you in my heart. I have learned
> so much this year that I could not
> have learned in any other way.

For that I am truly grateful.

Now I will go and try to recover
my health. The sandstorms and pollution
are wreaking havoc with my system. I
am particularly worried about my
ears which continually become
inflamed and infected. The tendon and
ligament tears that occurred at school
are not healing. So I will take some time to
let my body recover.

I wish you all the best, and will cherish
the relationships I had with you.

Love, Zanne

It was done. I left the surreal in the most surreal
way possible. Nervously, gratefully I flew to Izmir, the
third largest city in Turkey. I was picked up at the
airport by a man I had met briefly when I was at Mimi's
"farm" in February. He didn't speak any English and I
was operating on pure trust at this point. I did not
recognize where we were going because he took a
detour to pick up his teenage daughter. Then we headed
back into somewhat familiar territory and he dropped
me at the travel agency in Kusadasi.

Avril, Mimi's daughter who runs the office, was
not there when I arrived. (Mimi was out on tour and
would not be back in Kusadasi for close to a month.)
Five other employees were working in the townhouse-
turned-office, and graciously showed me to my room

upstairs. It was small and sunny with a balcony overlooking the backyard. A chunk of a Roman column lay abandoned on the ground. (Kusadasi is the jumping off point for Ephesus. Artifacts are continually unearthed even 12 miles away from the excavation site.) The bookkeeper worked in the other bedroom-turned-office. Jac was the number two office manager, a cook made two meals a day for everyone, and various other guides and drivers were in and out of the office. This was Mimi's extended "family." That extended family now included me. I was so grateful for this opportunity and also nervous about how I would, or would not, fit into the family dynamics.

The dear, shy cook served us all lunch outside under an umbrella. The food was simple and absolutely delicious. Fresh tomatoes, goat cheese, bread from the market and, of course, olives. It was a luxury to have someone take care of all the cooking and washing up. *I must have some good karma,* I thought to myself, *because this is straight out of a movie.* So much generosity and largesse was beyond my ken. The weather was beautiful, warm and sunny; the atmosphere relaxed. I could wear shorts, blue jeans, get back to my casual self. Flowers were in bloom everywhere, and we were within walking distance of the Aegean Sea. I had come out of the desert and landed in heaven.

Jac began showing me the computer I would use to book travel tours, answer questions and develop itineraries. I was in a whole new world, the world of travel, and there were a lot of details to learn. I'm a quick study, so I wasn't too worried. An hour or two after lunch, Avril arrived. She lived in a townhouse around the corner, and walked to work. The cook rustled up some food for her and she began to orient me to what I would be doing.

Avril told me she wanted the company to be a pleasant place to work. She had previously worked in a factory, and it was grim. She was dead set against working on weekends as she had in the factory. My work hours were to be from 11:00 AM to 7:00 PM, and I would have the house to myself on weekends and after work hours. She proudly showed me the TV she had gotten for me, offered to let me use a company car on weekends to see the sites, and said she was glad I was there. She had been waiting anxiously as their workload ramped up. She actually put off hiring someone new when the last person moved on, knowing I was on the way.

That worried me a bit; did she think I was staying long-term? I hastened to clarify that I would only be there two and a half months. That seemed to come as a surprise. The opportunities for misunderstanding were rife because my arrangements were organized through Mimi. I had not talked to Avril since booking my own travel in February; in fact, this was the first time we had ever met.

Avril gave me a thumb drive containing the tour company's website information, and asked me to create templates for the various tours that were available. This was a more complicated job than I had been expecting. The work required a lot of attention to detail, and I was just beginning to learn which details were important (all of them). I started to make templates. I was a little slow because I had to copy and resize a lot of photos, which I had never done before. Given that I had zero experience in the world of tour guiding, I felt I was learning quickly enough.

Avril talked with me about what I would do when I returned home. I told her I had a job waiting for me, but was beginning to fantasize about working for her from the United States. I was still desperately trying to find a way to live with less stress than I was encountering in schools. Although her company specializes in tours for Americans and Canadians, there were no native English speakers on staff. (Avril studied in the U.S., however, and she and Mimi spoke excellent English.)

My idea was received much more enthusiastically than I expected. Difficulties with time differences could be lessened; there was an annual convention in the States that Avril didn't like going to, though the company needed to maintain a presence. I might actually be able to provide useful service to the business.

Again, I counted my lucky stars. And buckled down to work. Serious tensions in the workplace soon became obvious. One day, Avril started screaming at Jac, saying that a mistake he made had lost them a lot of money. Another day, she asked me to get details about how the tour was going from one of the guides (her brother). She liked to send notes with specific anecdotes to the booking agents in the U.S. He responded that it was "nice." When I attempted to get details, he said, "Do you speak English?"

I replied that English was all I spoke. "Then you know what nice means." I didn't retort that nice was one of the most nondescript words in the English language. Avril was furious. She called her mother, her uncle, another brother, railing about this unacceptable behavior on the part of her brother. *Hmmm? Trouble in Paradise?*

212

I was soon fielding phone calls and got a question I didn't know how to answer yet. I told the caller that I was new. I would talk with someone more knowledgeable and get back to them right away. Avril was out of the office so I talked with Jac and asked him what to do. He said he would take care of it. Jac knew his way around the business, but his English was just developing. Communication was dicey, although I was learning to translate questions into Turkish on Google. In any case, about ten minutes later, Avril came swooping into the office, yelling at me for telling a client I was new. "You are 60 years old and you don't know not to do that!" Her diatribe went on for about twenty minutes. Finally when she began to calm down, I told her I had said I would get the information the client needed and get back to them as soon as possible.

Oh, that's not what Avril thought I had done; that was a perfectly acceptable response from her point of view. She thought I had smiled and said, "I can't help you." Click. She thanked me for letting her talk without interruption. She apologized and allowed as how she could be a bit emotional at times.

Out of the frying pan and into the fryer. I didn't leave Kuwait to be under the thumb of a different controlling, unreasonable person. But Avril did apologize, which is more than Mr. Khaled ever did. Maybe this was an isolated incident?

A few days went by. Avril asked me to stop working on templates and begin answering emails and generating itineraries. I learned the lodging and scheduling systems and began building itineraries. Evidence of Avril's petty tyranny mounted. The fear it inspired on the part of the other folks working in the office was palpable. Other things were not going as described either. I did not have the house to myself after 7 PM. Avril and Jac often worked very late into the night. There was a lot of noise, loud music, and arguments; hard on my quiet, woodchuck nature.

The weekend came. I walked down to Ladies' Beach on the Aegean, passing camels on the way. The beach was urban and crowded, the water as warm as a bathtub. I wandered through the tourist shops, walked out to an old castle. I marveled at the cruise ships, floating cities in their own right. Turkish men are great flirts; even at age 60, I got a lot of propositions. I also talked with a young shop owner and exchanged cultural tidbits that helped him with his customers. "All Americans think they are getting ripped off," I told him. "Searching for a bargain is an American sport." He had felt offended by their behavior because he thought they were questioning the worth of his goods. We planned to continue this dialogue while I was in Kusadasi.

Back at work, I continued to answer emails and develop itineraries. There were a million details, some of which I missed. None of the blunders resulted in loss of revenue, thank God. One day, Avril suggested I go to the farmers' market with the cook. We headed out and I was amazed at city block upon city block of fresh vegetables, piles of leaves (grape leaves for wrapping!), and household goods like clothespins. It was a market the size of an entire neighborhood. The vendors set up and tore down the stalls every single day. The cook remained quiet, but clearly knew exactly what to look for. It was wonderful to watch her unassuming competence.

I had been feeling for her because nobody ever thanked her for the food. If Avril and Jac were in the office late at night, they would cook, but not clean up.

By morning, the kitchen would be overrun with ants. The cook quietly cleaned up and started the next day's meals. The power differential was unmistakable. Although Avril took her responsibilities to her employees seriously, and sincerely wanted to help them, she was a tyrant. I was as kind as I knew how to be and did the work asked of me as quickly and accurately as possible.

But the other shoe was bound to drop. And it did, after I had been in Turkey for only nine days. Avril came in on Monday asking if the templates were done. I said, no, that I had switched to answering emails and developing itineraries individually as she had asked me to do. This was not acceptable to Avril. The work would go much faster if the templates were used. I agreed, but said that she had asked me to switch tasks and so I did.

"Well," Avril challenged, "why didn't you work all weekend to get them done?" I reminded her that she had told me she didn't want people to work on weekends. She lit into me again. "How dare you call yourself a Sufi. And there you are, all proper all the time."

Apparently being kind and considerate constituted faults in Kuwait *and* Turkey. After such similar confrontations at Shamiya School, I was not about to subject myself to this kind of treatment. I had been mistreated enough during my life. It was time to practice refusing abuse as often as necessary. "Don't worry," I told her, "this will not continue to be a problem for you. I'll catch a plane and leave tomorrow."

With the help of three other employees, who clearly understood and had experienced the wrath of Avril, I booked a flight to Washington State. I was suddenly aware of how common workplace abuse is in the private sector. Because I had worked in schools all my life, I had not been exposed to people throwing their weight around in such blatant ways. I felt heartsick for the others in the office; jobs were so scarce in Turkey that there was no way they could leave. They were stuck.

But I could leave, and I did, early the next morning. I was tired, shocked and disappointed. Life is not a movie, and my storybook stay in Turkey was not to be. I was learning that saying "No" to bad circumstances once is not enough. After years of acquiescing, I had some serious practice to do, and I exercised it with Avril. That exercise resulted in forfeiting $30,000; but staying and paying Avril's price would have cost me a great deal more.

Chapter 31

Ya Rahim, The Most Merciful, The Most Compassionate

Hudson Point, Port Townsend, Washington

When I reached JFK Airport in New York City, I called my friend/Friend Rebecca. She had agreed to rent me one of the two small houses on her property in Port Townsend. But she was expecting me in the middle of July, not May. "By any chance is your house empty, Rebecca? I'm in New York and will be in Washington tonight, but haven't figured out where I will stay."

"Yes, the house is free. Zanne, just come and you can move right in. There are a few weeks between now and when I was expecting you that I have booked guests. But we will find you another place to stay. By July 15th you will have the house all to yourself." I was saved!

My homecoming was sweet. When I left for

Kuwait I had felt disconnected from people. I came home to the realization that there are people in Port Townsend who genuinely love me. I felt welcomed, nurtured and grateful to be back in the States where things generally work as expected; at least in comparison.

My friend, Nora, and I sat on East Marrowstone Beach. From our beach chairs, we gazed at both Mount Baker and Mount Rainier. We watched a pair of eagles soar as boats plied the shipping lanes. Great blue herons raised their prehistoric wings to flap leisurely to shore. "You know," she said, "you had to go to Kuwait."

"What do you mean?"

"How could you resist the opportunity to go to a school that actually wanted your experience? Actually wanted to reform and improve things for students? I know it didn't turn out that way, but this had the potential to be a dream come true for you."

It was true. There was no way I could resist that chance, even knowing, as I did from the outset, that people don't always mean what they say.

After I returned I was often asked, "Was being a woman a factor in why things were so difficult in Kuwait?"

It was a question I didn't know how to answer. The culture definitely inhibits women tremendously, even though Kuwait is one of the most progressive of the Gulf States. But I was not a member of the culture and allowances were made. My behavior did not have to comply with the requirements an Arabic woman must follow.

Expectations within the school, however, were

completely different from what I anticipated. I was probably naïve to assume that the working environments in international schools would have similar values and procedures as American ones. We had a lot of female administrators at Shamiya School, but administrators, in general, were not expected to take initiative or responsibility. We were to follow instructions whether we were male or female. I brought a lot to the job – initiative, an ability to work independently as well as collaboratively, knowledge of best practices and high quality materials. I considered these valuable assets, but they felt like liabilities in Kuwait. The school was a thoroughly hierarchical organization controlled by a Board of Directors that had one goal – to make money. I suspect even the superintendent had very little power or authority.

In a lot of ways, though, Shamiya was not so different from American schools, except Americans are more subtle. The Kuwaitis were blatant in their efforts to control, and to make money. They didn't pay lip service to collaboration as we do in the U.S. And Middle Eastern cultures do not encourage independence. Instead, rules and decisions are expected to come out of sanctioned norms and customs; opinions are determined by an in-group. Disagreeing with someone publicly results in their losing face, which, in a society where honor is everything, is a grave social misstep. Solving problems without articulating what the difficulties are, without airing all possible viewpoints is beyond me. I'm not criticizing; I'm sure there are people who know how to do that. But even now, I can't picture what it would look like.

I suspect I would have needed a great deal more finesse to be effective in a Middle Eastern setting. In retrospect, it is easy to see where I stepped in the cultural soup, using western norms that were completely out of sync with my surroundings. It wasn't until months after my return that I realized how completely, though unwittingly, I had challenged the honor of the high school principal.

The principal had called a school-wide meeting, but our department was the only one to show up. She launched into an hour-long tirade about how poorly we were performing our supervisory duties at the various gates around the building. *At least we showed up for your meeting,* I thought to myself. Thinking back to (Western) readings about good leadership, I decided to support the staff. I stood and said, "Respectfully, we hear what you are saying. Could you tell us what you would like us to do differently?"

I was proud of myself – I shouldn't have been. The whole incident blew up in my face as the principal experienced my remarks as a full-on attack, in public, no less. Her criticisms toward our staff continued and intensified. I tried again, with less success from my point of view and more dishonor from hers. Our relationship was never the same.

Even in the States, my attempts to identify a problem with an eye toward solving it are rarely received well. People in the U.S. seem pathologically optimistic to me. Look at the Great Recession. Plenty of people in the banking world warned about the problems of bundling mortgages. The response they got: they were fired for not having a good attitude. (My new favorite T-shirt saying is, "I'm not a pessimist; I'm an optimist with experience.")

Recently, I read about a study in the book

Beautiful Souls: The Courage and Conscience of Ordinary People in Extraordinary Times, by Eyal Press. He cites the work of Philip Jos, Mark Tompkins, and Steven Hays in their study of whistleblowers.

"Whistleblowers," they concluded, "exhibit little of the cynicism and disillusionment that often go along with political activism or dissent. They are, if anything, too trusting of the organization's willingness to respond to their concerns." That would be me.

Press cited a survey which asked, "In general, would you say that people should obey the law without exception or are there exceptional occasions on which people should follow their consciences even if it means breaking the law?" Americans ranked dead last in 10 western nations in saying yes, they should follow the law. When asked if right and wrong "should be a matter of personal conscience," Americans overwhelmingly answered, "No."

This was not what I would have expected. I believed the overt messages I heard throughout my life that bad things happen when good people stay silent. For all our "rugged individualism" in the U.S., it turns out our culture values conformity above all. And yet, this explained a lot about the responses I encountered when trying to do the right thing for kids. The lack of enthusiasm for reform, continuous improvement, or talking about problems, have their roots in these unspoken values.

In the U.S., we say we care about our kids, but our budgets suggest otherwise. Education has become hopelessly politicized, and most decisions have a basis in money, not profit, necessarily, but money. (Unless you are in the educational testing and publishing

221

business where there are enormous profits to be made.) Our educational practices seldom reflect current research, and professional development has been lost to budget cuts. Don't get me started about the reorganization that should happen to address the cultural changes that have occurred in the U.S. over the course of my career. (For example, we could pull health and social services under the same roof as education. We could implement year-round school to decrease loss of academic skills over the long summer; start the high school day later to allow adolescent brains to be fully awake before expecting academic performance.)

And yet amidst all this chaos and contradiction, whether in the United States or Kuwait, some of the hardest working people are found in schools. Teachers subsidize education with their money, their blood, sweat and tears, and are seldom recognized for it. Because American society does not acknowledge the vastly different social/emotional challenges that students bring to school with them, teachers' working conditions have become more and more difficult. If you ever get a chance, thank a teacher.

When I left for Kuwait, I felt unassailable. I believed I lived with enough integrity that I would be protected from harm. In fact, I was assailed at every turn. I was assailed for getting things done, for being knowledgeable, for doing things I had not actually done, for being cheerful, of all things. Had the situation been reversed and I had been depressed, incompetent and ignorant, I still would have been assaulted.

There will probably always be people who want to be at war with me in some way. And the spoils of war are pain; pain, but not necessarily suffering. In order to cease suffering, I have to trust that I am enough; I have to trust that I am worthy of a good life; and I have to accept that others will not always agree with me, support me or like me. I have to live as a wave on the ocean that remains constant regardless of storm or calm. So much for the idea that if I work hard enough and earnestly enough, I will reach perfection and be loved by all. The death of a myth. Thank God!

Soon after returning home, I emailed my Sufi teacher and briefly told her about my experiences in Kuwait. She sent me back a new set of practices, the first change in 20 years, and evidence that the changes I felt in myself were real. It's always so hard to tell; that darn ego can co-opt just about anything, and adores hijacking spiritual striving for its own purposes.

My teacher suggested that I get in touch with another Sufi teacher in Seattle. "It's good to have friends along the way," she said. So I took the ferry into the city, and drove to a small house in a modest neighborhood. Wakil was in the backyard, which he and his wife, Guinevere, have turned into a sanctuary of peace and beauty. As we sat under the trees, I described some of the sea changes rippling through me.

I explained to Wakil how angry I had been with God. Despite all the enormous challenges I faced, I still had not found the joy I believed I deserved – the joy that was the essence of my soul. Wakil replied, "Who is this 'I' who was angry with God?" If there is only One Being, which I know to be the truth, I must have been mad at myself. I'm ready now to stop being angry; I'm ready now to be as gentle and forgiving with myself as I have always been with others.

It had been important to me to have work that gave back to the world. I took my responsibility to the children and families I worked with seriously. And I remain happy and fulfilled that I could be of service to so many people. At the same time, I don't need to be proud of the work I do … it is enough to do the best I can and not expect to change other people or the organizations in which I work. Attachment to professional pride contributed to the hubris and judgmentalism that barred the door to peace, contentment and joy.

Yes, it was definitely time to turn in my *Different Clan* ID badge. I realized I often made pre-emptive judgment strikes (quietly inside my head) on other people. This fed my need to be highly competent and, thus, worthy. My ego used excelling at the job as ammunition against other people. That is not a kind, compassionate way to view others. Andrew Solomon made a great observation in his book *Far From the Tree*, when describing a woman with a lot of trauma in her history: "… [She] is an idealist who lives to almost ostentatiously high standards, as if determined to outflank weakness and self-indulgence."

Oh, my God, I thought when I read that, *that's me!* I did not want life's slings and arrows to make me weak or self-indulgent. I suspect my attempts to protect myself from becoming weakened or paralyzed were a real pain in the ass to the people around me. I apologize to you all.

Yet back at work, I couldn't seem to give up those high standards. The truth is I don't really want to give them up because they improve what I do. Sometimes, as I worked part-time for the last two years before retirement, I echoed Angella's question, "Why do you care so much?"

Elie Wiesel has answers, "One must wager on the future. To save the life of a child, no effort is superfluous. To make a tired old man smile is to perform an essential task. To defeat injustice and misfortune, if only for one instant, for a single victim, is to invent a new reason to hope." I don't know how to teach without throwing myself all in. Moderation will not do. I need to live with Elie Wiesel's hope in my heart.

Sri Nisargadatta Maharaj says in *I Am That*, "The inclusive mind is love in action, battling against circumstances, initially frustrated, ultimately victorious." I want to cultivate an inclusive mind. When I can do that without expecting everyone else to live up to impossibly high standards, maybe I will really have something. I faithfully report that this is a work in progress.

But progress there is: I am ready to give up the hubris that I am in control of anything, including my own life. Viewed psychologically, the secondary trauma and accompanying depression I developed toward the end of my teaching career, which was exacerbated in Kuwait, may have served a vital role in this progress. In another brilliant book, *Noonday Demon*, Andrew Solomon writes, "A situation in which a person cannot disengage from a truly hopeless goal may be resolved through depression, which forces disengagement." My sense of commitment had bound me to many a hopeless situation. I consciously, gratefully sever that bond.

I now view life as a mystery to be explored rather than a problem to be solved. I look for guidance wherever I can find it, and I found a lot in Kuwait. Being outside my own culture provided me the freedom to look at my quiet life, and be happy and satisfied with it. I don't have to do, do, do all the time, even if my culture tells me to. And I don't have to fear anything. What a weight drops off when I no longer live in fear: fear of not having enough money, fear of not being right all the time, fear of not being enough, fear of, well, you name it. Loss of fear is true freedom.

Alan Jones wrote, "The desert is a symbol of two things: human extremity and God's self-giving. We need to be jolted out of our apparent self-sufficiency into the place of real need so God can give Himself to us." I journeyed to the desert of Kuwait out of desperation, and was hit by a thunderbolt whose light exposed my real need, and whose blessings will echo throughout the rest of my life.

Chapter 32

Ya Samad, The Satisfier of All Needs, The Eternal

Inspiration from Ephesus, Turkey

I was lost and found in Kuwait. I lost my identity as a valued professional. I found grace. I lost my cultural identification. I found joy. I lost the pride of my ego. I found peace of mind.

Nisargadatta says, "Obtuseness and wrong pursuits bring about a crisis and the disciple wakes up to his own plight. Wise is he who does not wait for a shock, which can be quite rude." Clearly I was not a wise person; I endured shock after shock in my life until finally the desert put my plight into stark relief. As a result, I was saved. "Saved from what?" Nisargadatta goes on. "From illusion. Salvation is seeing things as they are." Not as I want them to be, or think they should be, but as they are.

Expecting the world to conform to my personal needs, desires or beliefs is a recipe for misery. Why should the world conform to my view? I have no more access to Truth and Wisdom than anyone else. I am a soul living in a human body with all its beauties and limitations. No more, no less. I am an aspect of the One Being. No more, no less.

Nisargadatta explains that existence involves the pain of separation and limitation. If willing and able to be at one with that knowledge, however, I no longer need help to escape the pain. I am learning to live in that oneness. It doesn't always help me function day-to-day. Increased sensitivity makes everyday life more challenging than when I was blundering along thinking I could control it. But the control was nothing but illusion. In living that realization, peace and contentment sprout in the soil where disappointment previously grew.

What of help for others? "You can help another by precept and example and, above all, by your being," Nisargadatta continues. "You cannot give what you do not have and you don't have what you are not. You can only give what you are – and of that you can give limitlessly." Without trying to exact a particular outcome, I now exist and give whatever I am to whoever crosses my path.

Since returning from Kuwait, I experience the literal appearance on my doorstep of people who sense what I have. They search for what I gained in the fires of Kuwait and their ensuing Grace. I don't need to do anything, but something about our interactions feeds them.

An elderly, single woman living in the neighborhood rang my doorbell one day. We spent several days deep in conversation. I had never met her before. A stranger emailed me seeking information about my grandfather. He had been miraculously cured of encephalitis, with my grandfather as his attending physician – after he was declared dead on arrival at the hospital. Thus began a rich exchange of emails in which we explored our spiritual beliefs. Another long-time friend experiencing huge crisis in his life, found his way to me after many years. To this day, we are shoring up each others' souls.

It can be lonely abiding in this view of self as a reflection of the Divine Whole. It has a paradoxical effect on me; I am at once infinitely more compassionate and loving toward people *a n d* more detached from them. Often this loving detachment is a total mystery to others. More than that, it can occasionally seem callous. The friend whose parents are declining and nearing death does not understand my apparent lack of concern. My experience is one of joy and anticipation for those who will cross over into the next form of life. I know that we who are left behind will miss them, but they are going to be in ecstasy. How can I wish to delay that?

One of Nisargadatta's disciples said to him, "The *jnani* [the realized soul] seems to be a very lonely being, all by himself."

Nisargadatta replied, "He is alone, but he is all. He is not even a being. He is the being-ness of all beings. Not even that. No words apply. He is what he is, the ground from which all grows … I am as I am for no merit of mine, and they are as they are for no fault of theirs … What *is* is loveable. Love is not a result … it is the very ground of being."

229

It is vitally important that I not forget that "I am as I am for no merit of mine." What I have learned came to me as pure grace, unearned through work or virtue. After years of ridiculously earnest striving, I finally let go in Kuwait. When I did, a vast opening appeared, and into that opening stepped the Divine.

Not quite a year after returning from Kuwait, I went on a retreat entitled "Awakening the Healing Power of Joy" with Shahid, a senior Sufi teacher. I briefly described my experiences in Kuwait to him. "One year is not enough time to recover from what you have been through," he told me. "That could have killed you." He was not speaking metaphorically.

During the retreat, Shahid explained that joy is not an emotion, it is something much higher. For me joy is compatible with melancholy, with an aching love for the world and the people in it, with peace and contentment. Some of the melancholy arises out of the distance my worldview can put between me and others. This is part of the price I pay for walking the path that chose me. I accept that I don't go into the Great Mystery of Life on my own terms. It has Its own operating manual and I don't get to edit. In exchange, I experience being wrapped in love that originates in the Divine realm. Illumination is our natural state, if we can only get out of the way to welcome it in. We don't need to understand it all; just be curious about our experience.

So here I am, ensconced in the beautiful English garden that Rebecca created, walking the beach, and around the lagoon into wooded hills overlooking the Salish Sea. Joseph Campbell writes in *The Hero with a Thousand Faces*, "The returning hero, to complete his adventure, must survive the impact of the world ... The first problem ... is to accept as real, after an experience of the soul-satisfying vision of fulfillment, the passing joys and sorrows, banalities and noisy obscenities of life. Why re-enter such a world? Why attempt to make plausible, or even interesting, to men and women consumed with passion, the experience of transcendental bliss?"

Somehow I need to learn to walk easily in both the everyday world and the world of the spirit, crossing the boundary ceaselessly, seamlessly. As Campbell points out, "It is possible to speak from only one position at a time, but that does not invalidate the insights of the rest ... The individual ... no longer tries to live but willingly relaxes to whatever may come to pass in him ..."

I've always had difficulty relating to the petty passions of life. And my newfound realizations did not make that easier. I was drawn to contemplation and devotion upon my return; I had little interest in the workaday goings-on of the world.

As Nisargadatta says, "To affect the course of events I must bring a new factor into the world and the factor can only be myself, the power of love and understanding focused in me." And more, as if talking directly to me, "What business have you with saving the world when all the world needs is to be saved *from* you? Get out of the picture and see whether there is anything left to save." Who needs to hear that more than a member of the *Different Clan*?

As I prepare to retire, surrendering to whatever life sends my way, our culture pushes on me: "What will you do when you retire?" people ask me. This seems an absurd question to me – I'm going to not work! I am going to see what is around the corner. Why do I have

231

to make plans to do something? And yet in the everyday world this is a perfectly reasonable question. I have learned to say that I will write, make rugs, dance and sing. That seems to allay most people's concerns.

And then I have space to fulfill my life's purpose to love, and be a conduit of joy. Every single person on the face of the earth has access to a life of grace and illumination. It is our natural state. But there is more. As Pir Vilayat Inayat Khan writes, " ... the culmination of the soul's journey is not just returning to its original state. Instead, it is how the soul has evolved through its passage on earth: what meaning has been extracted from its experiences; ... the unique way each soul's unfoldment has contributed to the evolution of the Universe itself." I pursue my quiet path, knowing it to be part of the Universe's evolution. I wish you joy and peace as you pursue yours.

I leave you in the capable hands of Hafiz, translated by Daniel Ladinsky:

Now is the time
For you to deeply compute the impossibility
That there is anything
But Grace.

ABOUT THE AUTHOR

 ZANNE ALDER holds Master's Degrees in Educational Psychology and Social Work. She spent 40 years working in schools as a teacher, counselor, professional development trainer and, briefly, administrator. She also has extensive experience in outdoor education, adventure-based counseling and restorative justice. Alder lives on the shoulder of Lookout Mountain, just south of Bellingham, Washington, where she practices her Sufi meditations daily.

Made in the USA
San Bernardino, CA
21 June 2018